SUSTAINABILITY MANAGEMENT AND NETWORK MANAGEMENT

Japanese Management and International Studies
(ISSN: 2010-4448)

Editor-in-Chief: Kazuki Hamada *(Okayama Shoka University, Japan)*

Published

Vol. 20 *Sustainability Management and Network Management*
edited by Kazuki Hamada, Johei Oshita & Hiroshi Ozawa

Vol. 18 *Management Accounting for Healthcare*
edited by Takami Matsuo & Yoshinobu Shima

Vol. 17 *Management Control Systems for Strategic Changes:*
Applying to Dematurity and Transformation of Organizations
edited by Shufuku Hiraoka & Akimichi Aoki

Vol. 16 *Sustainability Management and Business Strategy in Asia*
edited by Katsuhiko Kokubu & Yoshiyuki Nagasaka

Vol. 15 *Fixed Revenue Accounting: A New Management Accounting Framework*
edited by Kenichi Suzuki & Bruce Gurd

Vol. 14 *Holistic Business Process Management: Theory and Practice*
edited by Gunyung Lee, Masanobu Kosuga & Yoshiyuki Nagasaka

Vol. 13 *Management of Innovation Strategy in Japanese Companies*
edited by Kazuki Hamada & Shufuku Hiraoka

Vol. 12 *Lean Management of Global Supply Chain*
edited by Yasuhiro Monden & Yoshiteru Minagawa

Vol. 11 *Entrepreneurship in Asia: Social Enterprise, Network and Grassroots*
Case Studies
edited by Stephen Dun-Hou Tsai, Ted Yu-Chung Liu, Jersan Hu &
Shang-Jen Li

Vol. 10 *Management of Enterprise Crises in Japan*
edited by Yasuhiro Monden

Vol. 9 *Management of Service Businesses in Japan*
edited by Yasuhiro Monden, Noriyuki Imai, Takami Matsuo &
Naoya Yamaguchi

Vol. 8 *Management of an Inter-Firm Network*
edited by Yasuhiro Monden

For the complete list of titles in this series, please go to
http://www.worldscientific.com/series/jmis

Japanese Management and International Studies – Vol. 20

SUSTAINABILITY MANAGEMENT AND NETWORK MANAGEMENT

editors

Kazuki Hamada
Okayama Shoka University, Japan

Johei Oshita
Kyushu University, Japan

Hiroshi Ozawa
Nagoya University, Japan

World Scientific

NEW JERSEY · LONDON · SINGAPORE · BEIJING · SHANGHAI · HONG KONG · TAIPEI · CHENNAI · TOKYO

Published by

World Scientific Publishing Co. Pte. Ltd.

5 Toh Tuck Link, Singapore 596224

USA office: 27 Warren Street, Suite 401-402, Hackensack, NJ 07601

UK office: 57 Shelton Street, Covent Garden, London WC2H 9HE

Library of Congress Cataloging-in-Publication Data

Names: Hamada, Kazuki, editor. | Oshita, Johei, editor. | Ozawa, Hiroshi, editor.
Title: Sustainability management and network management / editors, Kazuki Hamada,
    Okayama Shoka University, Japan, Johei Oshita, Kyushu University, Japan,
    Hiroshi Ozawa, Nagoya University, Japan.
Description: New Jersey : World Scientific, [2023] | Series: Japanese management and
    international studies, 2010-4448 ; vol 20 | Includes bibliographical references and index.
Identifiers: LCCN 2023010343 | ISBN 9789811272257 (hardcover) |
    ISBN 9789811272264 (ebook) | ISBN 9789811272271 (ebook other)
Subjects: LCSH: Social responsibility of business--Japan. | Sustainable development--Japan. |
    Industrial management--Japan. | Organizational behavior--Japan. | Cooperation--Japan.
Classification: LCC HD60.5.J3 S87 2023 | DDC 658.4/080952--dcundefined
LC record available at https://lccn.loc.gov/2023010343

British Library Cataloguing-in-Publication Data
A catalogue record for this book is available from the British Library.

For any available supplementary material, please visit
https://www.worldscientific.com/worldscibooks/10.1142/13306#t=suppl

Desk Editors: Sanjay Varadharajan/Pui Yee Lum

Typeset by Stallion Press
Email: enquiries@stallionpress.com

Printed in Singapore

Japan Society of Organization and Accounting (JSOA)

President
Makoto Tomo, Seijo University, Japan

Vice Presidents
Kazuki Hamada, Okayama Shoka University, Japan
Yoshiyuki Nagasaka, Konan University, Japan

Directors
Akimichi Aoki, Senshu University, Japan
Gunyung Lee, Niigata University, Japan
Shufuku Hiraoka, Soka University, Japan
Noriko Hoshi, Hakuoh University, Japan
Masahiro Hosoda, Rikkyo University, Japan
Masaaki Imabayashi, Mejiro University, Japan
Noriyuki Imai, International Professional University of Technology in
    Nagoya, Japan
Tomonori Inooka, Kokushikan University, Japan
Masanobu Kosuga, Kwansei Gakuin University, Japan
Takami Matsuo, Kobe University, Japan
Yoshiteru Minagawa, Nagoya Gakuin University, Japan
Hiroshi Obata, Hitotsubashi University, Japan
Yoshinobu Shima, Kindai University, Japan
Kenichi Suzuki, Meiji University, Japan

Mission of JSOA and Editorial Information

For the purpose of making a contribution to the business and academic communities, the Japan Society of Organization and Accounting (JSOA), is committed to publishing Japanese Management and *International Studies* **(JMIS), which is a refereed annual publication with a specific theme for each volume**.

The series is designed to inform the world about research outcomes of the new "Japanese-style management system" developed in Japan. However, as the series title suggests, it also promotes "International Studies" on the managerial competencies of various countries that include Asian countries as well as Western countries under the globalized business activities.

Research topics included in this series are management of organizations in a broad sense (including the business group or inter-firm network) and the accounting for managing the organizations. More specifically, topics include business strategy, business models, organizational restoration, corporate finance, M&A, environmental management, operations management, managerial & financial accounting, manager performance evaluation, reward systems. The research approach is interdisciplinary, which includes case studies, theoretical studies, normative studies and empirical studies, but emphasizes real world business.

Our JSOA's board of directors has established an editorial board of international standing. In each volume, guest editors who are experts on the volume's special theme serve as the volume editors. The details of JSOA is shown in its by-laws contained in the home-page: http://jsoa.sakura.ne.jp/english/index.html.

© 2023 World Scientific Publishing Company
https://doi.org/10.1142/9789811272264_fmatter

Editorial Board

Preface

Sustainability means conducting activities from the perspectives of preserving the environment, society, and economy. These activities are broad and include not only companies but also national and local governments, non-profit organizations, and individuals. However, this volume aims to consider the problem from the standpoint of corporate management. To this end, in this volume, we would like to consider that "sustainability management not only earns profits, but also fulfills social responsibilities while considering the environment, people, and society, and enables management to continue to have the potential to survive in the future." In that sense, it is also related to the Sustainable Development Goals. However, we would like to consider aspects that companies have traditionally aimed for, e.g., corporate social responsibility management.

However, there are various approaches to sustainability management. In this volume, we focus mainly on employment issues within the company and networks for coexistence with business partners, customers, and residents, among others. In addition, companies need to aim for sustainability in collaboration with other companies and national and local governments. Therefore, we would like to consider this issue in this volume as well.

This volume consists of three parts. In Part 1, we would like to consider various aspects of the theory and points to note for implementing sustainability management. We would especially like to build a business model where sustainability factors are taken into consideration. Then, when implementing the business model, we will consider how to implement governance control, management functions and performance evaluation methods while increasing employee satisfaction.

In Part 2, we would like to examine the current state of sustainability management in Japanese companies based on data and examples, and to explore future development directions. We would particularly like to analyze the time productivity of employees as a factor to judge whether sustainability management is implemented efficiently, examine the examples of two manufacturing companies and two service companies, and analyze the data.

When implementing sustainability management, it is necessary to cooperate with other companies, cooperate with various stakeholders surrounding the company, and create a network for coexistence. Therefore, in Part 3, we would like to consider supply chain management as cooperation among companies, and how the private sector should cooperate with the public sector such as local governments.

Kazuki Hamada
November 15, 2022

About the Editors

Kazuki Hamada is a Professor in the Faculty of Business Administration at the Okayama Shoka University, Japan. He is also the Vice President of the Japan Society of Organization and Accounting. He has a Ph.D. in Management Science and Engineering from University of Tsukuba, Japan.

His current main research themes include sustainable management, innovation management, and inter-company supply chain management from the view of management accounting.

Professor Hamada has several publications to his credit, including the following: "Strategic Management and Profit Creation in the Context of Innovation: The Management of Innovation Value Chains," in Hamada, K. and Hiraoka, S., eds., *Management of Innovation Strategy in Japanese Companies*, World Scientific Publishing Co. Pte. Ltd., 2017; "Management Accounting Information for Consolidated Group Management," in Hamada, K., ed., *Business Group Management in Japan*, World Scientific Publishing Co. Pte. Ltd., 2010; "Total Productivity Management and the Theory of Constraints: An Integrated Application of Supply Chain Management Methods," in Monden, Y., *et al.*, eds., *Japanese Management Accounting Today*, World Scientific Publishing Co. Pte. Ltd., 2007; "Managerial Roles of Financial and Non-financial Measures in Supply Chain and Engineering Chain Management," in Monden, Y., *et al.*, eds., *Value-Based Management of Rising Sun*, World Scientific Publishing Co. Pte. Ltd., 2006; "A Method for Simultaneously Achieving Cost Reduction and Quality Improvement," and "A Management System for the Simultaneous Attainment of Customer Satisfaction and Employee Satisfaction," in Monden, Y., ed., *Japanese Cost Management*, Imperial College Press, 2000.

Johei Oshita is a Professor, Emeritus, Kyushu University, Japan. He has a Ph.D. in Economics from Kyushu University, Japan.

His current main research themes include French management accounting, French management control, and governance control theory.

Professor Oshita has several publications to his credit, including the following: "Yasuhiro Monden: Toyota Production System and Total Cost Management," in Sponem, S. and Pezet, A., eds., *Les Grands Auteurs en Contrôle de Gestion*, Editions EMS, 2nd ed., 2021; *Modern French Management Accounting*, Chuou-keizai sha, 2009 (in Japanese); "The Basic Idea of French Analytical and Management Accounting: A Comparative Analysis of Management Accounting in France, The U.S. and Japan," in Monden, Y., *et al.*, eds., *Value-Based Management of the Rising Sun*, World Scientific Publishing Co. Pte. Ltd., 2006; "The Great Authors of Management Control in Japan," in Bouquin, H., ed., *Les Grands Auteurs en Contrôle de Gestion*, Editions EMS, 2005; and "La Comptabilité de Gestion au Japon: Une Approche Historique," *Journal of Political Economy* (Society of Political Economy, Kyushu University), 1994.

Hiroshi Ozawa is a Professor in the Graduate School of Economics at the Nagoya University, Japan. He has a Ph.D. in Economics from Nagoya University.

His current main research themes include multidimensional business analysis, lean production system, innovation, and risk management from the view of management accounting.

Professor Ozawa has several publications to his credit, including the following: "Balancing Sales Needs with Supply Chain Needs: Production Control as the Arbiter" (with Jeffery K. Liker), *International Journal of Lean Enterprise Research*, 2015; "How to Maintain the Bargaining Position Defined in Toyota's Dealership Control," in Hamada, K., ed., *Business Group Management in Japan*, World Scientific Publishing Co. Pte. Ltd., 2010; "A Framework for Performance Evaluation Methods in Continual Improvement Activities," in Monden, Y., *et al.*, eds., *Japanese Management Accounting Today*, World Scientific Publishing Co. Pte. Ltd., 2007; and "Principles of Increased Productivity through Cell-Based Assembly," in Monden, Y., *et al.*, eds., *Value-Based Management of Rising Sun*, World Scientific Publishing Co. Pte. Ltd., 2006.

List of Contributors

Yuri Fukaya, Meiji University, Japan
Kazuki Hamada, Okayama Shoka University, Japan
Soichiro Higashi, Chiba Institute of Technology, Japan
Shufuku Hiraoka, Soka University, Japan
Noriyuki Imai, International Professional University of Technology in Nagoya, Japan
Aiko Kageyama, Hiroshima International University, Japan
Ayuko Komura, Kanagawa University, Japan
Yoshiteru Minagawa, Nagoya Gakuin University, Japan
Kazuyoshi Morimoto, Hagoromo University of International Studies, Japan
Miyabi Nashiba, Meiji University, Japan
Johei Oshita, Kyushu University, Japan
Hiroshi Ozawa, Nagoya University, Japan
Kenichi Suzuki, Meiji University, Japan
Kozo Suzuki, Bureau of Waterworks, Tokyo Metropolitan Government, Japan
Misato Tanaka, Meiji University, Japan
Runa Tsushima, Meiji University, Japan

Contents

Japan Society of Organization and Accounting (JSOA)   v

Editorial Board   ix

Preface   xi

About the Editors   xiii

List of Contributors   xvii

Part 1   Business Model and Control System for Sustainability Management   **1**

Chapter 1   Building and Managing Business Models That Emphasize Sustainability: How to Manage Economic and Social Values in Relation to Each Other   3

Kazuki Hamada

Chapter 2   Governance Control Initiatives and Challenges: Connecting the Board of Directors and Control Theory   19

Johei Oshita

Chapter 3   The Function of Top Management in This Age of Sustainability   39

Kazuyoshi Morimoto

Chapter 4   Multi-objective Corporate Behavior Model
               for Sustainable Management: Evaluation
               Method and the Selection and Search
               for a Solution   55
               Hiroshi Ozawa

**Part 2   Practical Examples of Sustainability Management
            in Japan   69**

Chapter 5   The Study of Japanese Companies' Per Hour
               Labor Productivity   71
               Shufuku Hiraoka

Chapter 6   Japanese Cost Management Based on Respect
               for the Humanity of Employees: The Case
               of Toyota   83
               Noriyuki Imai

Chapter 7   Study on Semiconductor Production Equipment
               Companies' ROESG Management   95
               Soichiro Higashi

Chapter 8   Healthcare Organizations and Sustainability:
               Current Situations and Challenges   111
               Aiko Kageyama

Chapter 9   Diversity Management Outcomes: Quantitative
               Verification of the Climate for Inclusion
               in the Japanese Hotel Industry   125
               *Misato Tanaka, Yuri Fukaya, Runa Tsushima,
               Miyabi Nashiba, Ayuko Komura,
               and Kenichi Suzuki*

Part 3 Network Management for Symbiosis **139**

Chapter 10 Management Accounting for Digital Twin-Driven
New Product Development in a Sustainable
Supply Chain   141

Yoshiteru Minagawa

Chapter 11 The Effects of Compliance on Sustainable
Management in Japanese Waterworks Utilities   161

Kozo Suzuki

Index   177

Part 1

Business Model and Control System for Sustainability Management

Chapter 1

Building and Managing Business Models That Emphasize Sustainability: How to Manage Economic and Social Values in Relation to Each Other

Kazuki Hamada

Okayama Shoka University, Okayama, Japan

1. Introduction: Attention to Sustainability Management and Its Benefits

Traditionally, the corporate goal has been to maximize profits, and social responsibility has been fulfilled through the resulting profit sharing and tax payments. There is supposed to be a tradeoff between the pursuit of profit (pursuit of economic value) and the solution of social problems, given that the legal regulatory requirements are met at a minimum. However, in recent years, sustainability management, which aims to improve the sustainability of businesses, has been attracting attention from the three broad perspectives of environment, society, and economy, particularly, because of the following reasons:

(1) increasing need to explore new growth areas after the maturation of existing markets,
(2) increasing skepticism about excessive pursuit of profits,

(3) tightening of regulations on environmental and social issues,
(4) responding to diverse demands of stakeholders.

The merits of executing sustainability management are as follows:

(1) It is possible to develop a competitive strategy in an advantageous manner. This is because products and services incorporating the concept of sustainability can increase their value by taking the environment and society into consideration. In addition, awareness that it is a product of the company that contributes to society improves customer loyalty. Sometimes, it is possible to reduce costs by reducing waste. As a result, it is possible to increase sales and reduce costs.
(2) Employees will become aware that they are contributing to society. This will motivate them to be more productive and improve employee satisfaction. As a result, it is possible to reduce costs and increase sales.
(3) The reliability of products and services increases, and transaction risk caused by distrust, especially transaction risk with supply chain members, decreases. Therefore, favorable transaction conditions can be obtained and the reputation of the company can be enhanced. As a result, it is possible to reduce costs and increase sales.
(4) It is possible to attract investors with high social awareness. As a result, it becomes possible to reduce the cost of raising capital.

However, the execution of sustainability management often involves the sacrifice of economic value. Therefore, in sustainability management, it is important to build a business model by relating economic and social value. In addition, it is important to consider effective materiality analysis methods, execution organizations, and human resources strategies in the construction of business models. The purpose of this chapter is to examine these points and propose effective management methods.

2. Concept of Economic Value and Social Value in Sustainability Management

2.1 *Economic value and social value*

First, I will consider the relationship between economic value and social value, which is a prerequisite for building a business model.

The economic value being referred to in this chapter pertains to the profit obtained from corporate activities or the financial value obtained as an evaluation thereof.

The social value covers aspects, such as profit distribution to stakeholders, human rights and local communities, impact on the global environment, and corporate governance mechanisms. This value consists of contributions that directly affect people, society, and the environment, through the actions of the company. It also includes the impact value that is created by influencing the solutions of social and environmental issues, beyond the direct impact (Business Policy Forum, 2020). However, there exists no unified view on the content of social value, and it is difficult to evaluate it. Impact Weighted Accounts (IWA), Value Balancing Alliance (VBA), International Accounting Standards Board (IASB), etc. are working on the evaluation methods for social value.

2.2 *Three ways of thinking about sustainability management*

Regarding sustainability management, there are three basic ideas:

(1) The idea that the pursuit of social value is one of the factors that bring about economic value: In the past, to improve economic value, it was emphasized that companies should carry out activities that do not have a negative impact on society and the environment. They are defensive risk-hedging measures. However, to improve economic value, aggressive measures that positively impact society and the environment and strengthen competitiveness must also be included.

(2) The idea of expanding the total sum (integrated value) of economic value and social values: In other words, the purpose of a company is not only the pursuit of economic value but also social contribution. Therefore, even if economic value declines, there can be an increase in social value.

(3) The idea of creating synergistic effects between economic value and social value by focusing on business activities through which both effects can be achieved: This is the idea that Porter and Kramer (2010) call Creating Shared Value (CSV) management. This management differs from (1), as it proposes only those activities in which the products and services provided by the businesses directly influence social problems and lead to their solutions.

The second idea, (2), seems to be problematic from the standpoint of an individual company, as it considers economic and social values to be equal. It considers that, in the extreme, there is no problem with activities in which economic value does not increase, as long as social value increases. For a company, social activities need to generate more economic value or reduce negative economic value.

The third idea, (3), proposes that the business activities should target only those areas that satisfy both economic and social aspects. Although such areas do exist, most of these areas targeted by strategy require the resolution of economic and social tradeoffs. Therefore, aiming for (3) as a strategy is too optimistic, and it is better to aim for it, if possible. However, it is necessary to actively explore such areas.

In reality, the first idea, (1), seems to be the most suitable. However, as mentioned above, activities that do not have negative impacts and activities that have positive impacts, on society and the environment as social activities, should be actively considered over the activities that solely have impacts on economic value. In other words, it is necessary to have positive strategies for society and the environment, instead of passive strategies. Additionally, it is important to create a mechanism in which social activities generate economic value and, conversely, a mechanism in which economic activities generate social value (Okada, 2015; Eccles and Serafeim, 2013; Serafeim, 2020). To that end, cooperation with non-profit organizations, governments, local governments, and supply chain members is also necessary.

3. Characteristics of Sustainability-Oriented Business Model

3.1 *Necessity of building a business model*

It is necessary to build a business model to concretely realize sustainability management. Professors Konno and Takai (2012, p. 334) said, "A business model is a series of business mechanisms for providing products to customers based on a formulated strategy and making a profit as a business." In addition, Johnson, Christensen, and Kagermann (2008) stated that business models consist of the following four elements: (1) customer value proposition (selecting customers to be targeted and clarifying the value to be provided), (2) profit equation (how to attain profit), and to achieve them (3) important resources and (4) important processes. All of these four elements are related to each other.

All business model definitions have one common aspect. Based on the theory of value creation, a mechanism for delivering value to customers and a profit (economic value) model for securing consideration are important. A business model is usually a mechanism that brings profits, but its crafting may include sustainability purposes other than profits. If the purpose of a business model is to generate profits, sustainability-oriented models may achieve these goals while taking sustainability factors into consideration. Therefore, even if a company's ultimate goal is to achieve economic value, this chapter supports the latter position.

3.2 *Considerations of business model construction and formulation process*

When building a business model, important sustainability issues may or may not be addressed by the business strategy itself. In the former case, solving social issues is a business opportunity, and the condition of shared value, as presented by Porter and Kramer (2010) is satisfied. In the latter case, it is necessary to implement the business strategy while solving sustainability issues. Apart from business strategy, issues exist in meeting the expectations of stakeholders, for example, issues such as consideration of human rights and diversity, employee safety, product safety, fair business practice, and environmental awareness. In this case as well, to increase its economic value, a company must not only reduce business risks by fulfilling the demands of stakeholders but also explore the possibilities of cost reduction, reputation enhancement, and creation of business opportunities.

As mentioned by Porter and Kramer (2006), there are three points in building a business model. The first point is to consider the combination of products and markets. Careful consideration of existing markets will allow us to see if it is possible to stay and which markets have the potential to differentiate. By constantly searching for social needs, new products and services may be discovered. The second point is to assess the supply chain process. A company's supply chain is the process of realizing profits, and by examining this process, it is possible to realize the origins of business opportunities and improvements. In addition, because the supply chain affects various social issues such as the natural environment, product safety, and working conditions, examining it can prevent social and environmental risks. The third point is to thoroughly study the situation in which company is based. Because the success of a company often depends on the existence of local companies and infrastructure, it is important to consider whether forming cluster can be advantageous for business development in the local community. To that end, it is necessary to maintain an open and transparent market and create a system that facilitates cooperation.

The ultimate goal of the business model discussed in this chapter is to improve economic value and, in the process of achieving it, also attain non-economic goals by conducting social activities that take sustainability factors into consideration. The following is a description of the formulation process with reference to the research by H. Chesbrough (2003):

(1)   Clarify the value proposition.
(2)   Find a market segment.
(3)   Clarify the structure of the corporate value chain.
(4)   Clarify the evaluation of potential profits and the sustainability factors that affect them, based on the value proposition and value chain.
(5)   Determine own company position within the value network, including suppliers, customers, competitors, and complements.
(6)   Establish competitive strategies to outperform competitors.

4. Importance of Materiality Analysis for Value Proposition

4.1 *Significance of value proposition*

In the process of formulating the abovementioned business model, it is especially important to clarify the value proposition, (1), as mentioned in the previous section. Value proposals offer economic value and social value. The value chain and value network also include both of these values. Mitsubishi Chemical Holdings Corporation manages to increase its value created on the basis of the three pillars of sustainability, innovation, and finance (economic efficiency) forming the "KAITEKI value (corporate value)" (Business Policy Forum, 2020). As ratios of evaluation, sustainability, innovation, and financial factors are set to 1:1:8. The value created through sustainability and innovation will ultimately lead to higher economic value.

If sustainability issues are included in the value proposition, the effects of their issues will appear in the medium to long term; therefore, it is important to examine the medium- to long-term consequences. In addition, all issues need to be derived from the corporate philosophy and purpose (meaning of existence), and proposals based on sustainability issues are especially important. Therefore, for value proposition, the following two points are required:

(1) long-term trend analysis, clarification of corporate philosophy, and clarification of purpose,
(2) formulation of long-term vision and introduction of backcasting.

Backcasting is a method to search for the materialities (important issues) that should be addressed now, to attain goals in the future. Therefore, by developing such strategies, it is possible to manage the dual-edged axes of medium- to long-term and short-term goals.

4.2 *Materiality analysis*

Materiality is an important issue that must be addressed to sustain a business model and improve corporate value in the short, medium, and long terms (Tsuchiya, 2020). The materialities vary by industry, business area, strategy, and corporate environment. Therefore, to effectively use the limited resources and increase economic value while satisfying sustainability goals, the identification of the materialities and efforts to focus on them are important.

It is necessary to select materialities that emphasize the characteristics of the company because they determine whether a competitive advantage can be achieved. It is possible to increase profits (cash flow), reduce risks, and respond to social issues by selecting important materialities and acting in accordance with them. This will also improve the reputation of companies and reduce the cost of raising capital. As a result, an increase in economic and social value, and ultimately a medium- to long-term increase in economic value, will be achieved.

As mentioned above, materialities pose social and environmental issues that can be resolved through business strategies. They can also address the social and environmental issues that cannot be resolved by business strategies. Therefore, it is necessary to consider these two aspects. At OMRON Corporation, factory automation, healthcare, mobility, and energy management have been set as the former issues focusing on sustainability. Materialities related to human resources, manufacturing environment, risk management, etc. have been set as the latter issues (Business Policy Forum, 2020).

5. Implementation of Sustainability Management and the Importance of Human Resources Strategy

5.1 *Points to consider in business management*

If a business model that takes sustainability into consideration can be built, it can be executed. Therefore, the following issues must be resolved before execution:

(1) Issues in building a business management system
     Sustainability management aims at its medium- to long-term spans, but the management span of the business divisions is short-termed. Therefore, it is necessary to build a management system to address these differences. In addition, sustainability-oriented activities are characterized by unclear and difficult goal-setting, especially in the incorporation and implementation of activities. Even if sustainable goals are set, many of them are not evaluated through common indicators, such as financial figures. In such a situation, it is important for the head office and business departments to cooperate.
     However, to increase the effectiveness of collaboration, it is necessary to determine the key performance indicators (KPIs) related to medium- to long-term profit materialities. It is then necessary to incorporate the set KPIs into the business plan of each department and continuously execute and monitor it. It is also necessary to disclose the KPIs of the business model to stakeholders, receive feedback on the information, and create a mechanism to incorporate the feedback into the strategy.

(2) Issues in the execution of management activities
It is necessary to clarify who makes and executes the sustainability-oriented decisions. It is also necessary to appoint a chief executive officer to the management council and assign a sustainability manager to work with the business units. For sustainability activities to be effective, relating them to the compensation system is also important. At OMRON Corporation, sustainability achievement is included in the determinants of executive compensation (Ibuki and Fukai, 2017).

(3) Social and environmental considerations in the supply chain
Since corporate activities involve not only a single company but also the related companies, it is necessary to meet the social and environmental demands of the entire supply chain. For example, they are requests for the natural environment at the raw material production area of suppliers and the working environment at the production site of them. In many cases, the implementation of sustainability management does not improve social value, unless it considers the demands of parties other than the company itself.

5.2 *Importance of human resources strategy*

The above points are important, but it is the employees who work in the company, and they play a central role in creating corporate value. Therefore, human resources strategy is most important for value creation. The Human Resources Report edited by Ito proposes a 3 Perspectives/5 Common Factors (3P/5F) model to characterize human resources strategies for sustainable corporate value improvement (Ministry of Economy, Trade and Industry, 2020).

3P emphasizes the following points:

(1) Is the human resources strategy linked to the management strategy?
(2) Is there a grasp on the gap between the business model or management strategy and the current human resources strategy?
(3) In the process of implementing the human resources strategy, are changes being promoted in the behaviors of organizations and individuals, establishing them as a part of the corporate culture?

5F contains the following factors:

(1) In building a human resources portfolio, the aim should be to diversify individuals and enable them to play active roles toward the realization of the business model and management strategy.
(2) An environment where individual diversity leads to dialog, innovation, and outcomes should be created.
(3) The skill gaps between aims of the future and the present should be skillfully filled.
(4) Diverse individuals should be encouraged to work independently and enthusiastically.
(5) A work style that is independent of time and place should be created.

The report points to a transformational direction for talent management, and the most important of these points seems to be employee engagement. In employee engagement, the relationship between a company and employees stands on an equal footing rather than a hierarchical relationship, and all components of the company grow together (Iwamoto, 2021).

6. How to Manage the Economic and Social Value Creation Process

6.1 *Usefulness of management control system*

To carry out sustainability management effectively and efficiently, management control is required. In the past, management control was mainly administered by management accounting methods as an aid to the execution of strategies. However, it has come to be managed by the entire control package including various control means exercising the expansion of its purpose and scope. In addition to traditional management accounting methods, management control includes control by control structure, organizational structure, elements of policy/procedure, and organizational culture (Ito, 2019).

For sustainability management, it is important to incorporate sustainability factors into the management control system. It is also necessary to respond to the demands of various stakeholders in addressing sustainability issues because the resolution of such issues does not directly lead to financial results. In these situations, interorganizational tensions rise. Smith and Lewis (2011) list the following potential forms of tensions:

(1) execution tension, which occurs at the level of executing various goals,
(2) organizational tension, which occurs when utilizing appropriate management methods for goals,
(3) affiliation tension, which is caused by organizational goals and values,
(4) learning tension, which is caused by existing knowledge and the need for further study.

They also state that resolving tensions is important.

Many researchers are studying how to use the belief system, boundary system, diagnostic control system, and interactive control system, advocated by Simons (1995), to solve these tensions. According to researchers, interactive control system is the most effective among others. Additionally, it is important to use various management methods together for tension dissolution.

6.2 *Management with balanced scorecards*

Regardless of the management method used to effectively implement a sustainability-oriented strategy, the objectives must be expressed as concrete numerical targets. The balanced scorecard (BSC) is one of the central management methods. BSC is a strategic management method that aims to achieve target measures from the four perspectives of finance, customer, business process, learning, and growth (Kaplan and Norton, 1992). Considering sustainability issues, they must be included in one of the four perspectives or introduced as a fifth perspective.

With BSC, sustainability can be related to the overall strategy and linked with business results. This will facilitate the penetration of sustainability strategies within the company and enable the formation of company-wide consensus, promoting communication within the company.

However, there are disadvantages to using BSC for sustainability strategies (Higashida, 2017):

(1) BSC is financially oriented, and ultimately only strategies that affect financial results are emphasized, even though there are many sustainability goals that are not related to financial results.
(2) BSC targets and measures are expressed numerically. However, the relationship between the leading measures and the resulting measures of sustainability cannot always be expressed numerically.
(3) Sustainability issues from the social perspective are not considered in traditional BSC.

If it is a for-profit company, it cannot be denied that financial results are highly prioritized, but it is necessary to use BSC in consideration of other issues. It is also necessary to select appropriate measures that address sustainability issues and devise appropriate measures for social and environmental constraints and risk requirements. Some sustainability measures have positive impacts and some have negative impacts. Considering the complex relationships between the sustainability measures is also important.

Figure 1 shows the four perspectives of BSC by dividing them into those related to economic value and those related to social value.

Materiality analysis is used to determine the appropriate measures to address the important issues, and they are used as the central measures of each of the four perspectives. In addition, the incidental measures that must be strategically achieved are determined and they are added to the four perspectives. Subsequently, the causal relationships between the measures are considered for executing the strategy, and each target value is then set. It is important to devise a management system in which two types of activities interact, just as the activities aimed at economic value promote the achievement of social value, and the activities aimed at social value promote the achievement of economic value. They should be combined with consistent human strategies. It is also necessary to devise measures to improve social value so that business risk can be reduced, the

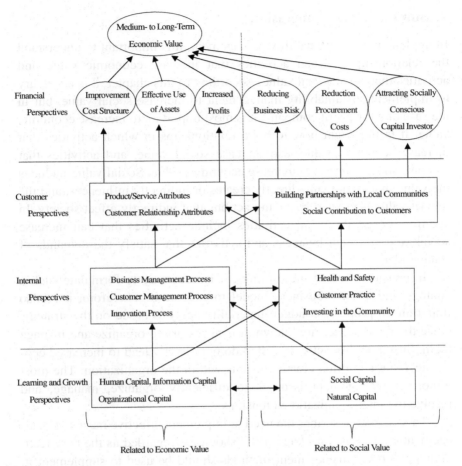

Figure 1. Conceptual Diagram for Determining Important BSC Measures

cost of raising capital can be reduced, and investors with high social awareness can be attracted.

To achieve strategic goals, it is important to focus on the BSC management method and to use it as the technique of interactive control and diagnostic control. Other means such as belief system, boundary system, administrative control, and organizational culture should also be used to exercise comprehensive control.

7. Summary and Conclusion

In implementing sustainability management, it is important to understand the relationship between activities that increase economic value and activities that boost social value. According to this chapter, it is necessary to implement sustainability management to increase social value, but in the case of a for-profit company, it is most important to increase economic value. It is important how to build relationships in which activities that increase economic value also increase social value, and activities that increase social value also increase economic value. Social value includes the value that a company directly creates or indirectly influences, and the impact value is created by taking actions that indirectly affect society. In addition, corporate social activities include activities that can increase social value through business and activities that satisfy the demands of stakeholders.

In consideration of these things, it is necessary to formulate such a strategy and build a business model to execute it. Therefore, it is also important to properly conduct materiality analysis based on the strategy. Once the materialities are known, it is necessary to organize and manage them. Sustainability activities often do not directly lead to increased economic value and often create tensions within the organization. The most important management issue is to efficiently organize, manage, and resolve the interorganizational tensions.

This chapter describes the need to implement effective means of management control as a package. BSC should be regarded as the core technique, and other management methods should be used to supplement it. BSC is also important to exercise diagnostic control, but it seems to be particularly important in administering interactive control and trial learning.

Successful companies in Japan have long aimed for sustainability management that also considers social value, in line with the Japanese style of management. It is necessary to consider new methods of sustainability management by making use of the strong on-site capabilities and building cooperative relationships that utilize Japanese corporate affiliates on the basis of Japanese culture and values.

References

Business Policy Forum (2020). Survey Report on "Expectations for 'Social Value' Created by Companies to Achieve SDGs," Business Policy Forum, Japan, March (in Japanese).

Chesbrough, H. (2003). *Open Innovation: The New Imperative for Creating and Profiting from Technology*, Boston: Harvard Business School Press.

Eccles, R. G. and Serafeim, G. (2013). Performance Frontier: Innovating for a Sustainable Strategy, *Harvard Business Review*, May.

Higashida, A. (2017). Integration of Sustainability in Strategy: Current Situation and Challenges in Sustainability Control System Research, *Meijo Ronso*, March (in Japanese).

Ibuki, E. and Fukai, K. (2017). Deepening Sustainability Management and Operations, *Titekisisan-sozo*, December (in Japanese).

Ito, K. (2019). *Management Control to Create an Organization*, Tokyo: Chuokeizai-sha (in Japanese).

Iwamoto, T. (2021). *A Study on Sustainable Corporate Value Improvement and Human Resources Strategy: Utilization of Employee Engagement for Corporate Management and Its Promotion Measures*, Japan Public Affairs Association, February (in Japanese).

Johnson, M. W., Christensen, C. M., and Kagermann, H. (2008). Reinventing Your Business Model, *Harvard Business Review*, December.

Kaplan, R. S. and Norton, D. P. (1992). The Balanced Scorecard: Measures that Drive Performance, *Harvard Business Review*, **70**(1).

Konno, Y. and Takai, F. (2012). *Core Text: Innovation Management*, Tokyo: Shinseisha (in Japanese).

Ministry of Economy, Trade and Industry (2020). *Study Group Report on Sustainable Improvement of Corporate Value and Human Capital: Human Resources Version Ito Report*, Ministry of Economy, Trade and Industry, September (in Japanese).

Okada, M. (2015). The Whereabouts of New Companies: Does CSV Lead to Competitive Advantage?, *Diamond Harvard Business Review*, January (in Japanese).

Porter, M. R. and Kramer, M. R. (2006). Strategy and Society: The Link Between Competitive Advantage and Corporate Social Responsibility, *Harvard Business Review*, December.

Porter, M. R. and Kramer, M. R. (2010). Creating Shared Value, *Harvard Business Review*, January–February.

Serafeim, G. (2020). Social-Impact Efforts That Create Real Value, *Harvard Business Review*, September–October.

Simons, R. (1995). *Levers of Control: How Managers Use Innovative Control Systems to Drive Strategic Renewal*, Harvard Business School Press.

Smith, W. K. and Lewis, M. W. (2011). Toward a Theory of Paradox: A Dynamic Equilibrium Model of Organizing, *Academy of Management Review*, **36**(2).

Tsuchiya, D. (2020). *Points of Materiality Analysis: Toward Improving Corporate Value*, Tokyo: KPMG/Azusa, Japan (in Japanese).

Chapter 2

Governance Control Initiatives and Challenges: Connecting the Board of Directors and Control Theory

Johei Oshita

Kyushu University, Fukuoka, Japan

1. Introduction

Corporate governance reform has become a significantly heated topic in recent years, especially owing to reforms in the "board of directors" system of publicly listed companies. The debates surrounding corporate governance reform differ from existing arguments on corporate governance. They weigh the proper approach to companies' institutional design — the configuration and function of the board of directors — particularly in terms of role expectations of independent outside directors. They also focus on and clarify the perspective of "offensive governance," which promotes healthy entrepreneurship, facilitates sustainable corporate growth, and enables mid- and long-term improvement in corporate value rather than adopting defensive approaches characterized by avoidance of risks and prevention of misconduct. These points share commonalities with the notion of "controlling the governance" addressed and focused on in this chapter.

We begin by grounding the discussion in the French concept of paradoxes in control and focus on business model as a means to mitigate these paradoxes (Bouquin and Kuszla, 2013). Especially, the paradoxical nature of control is recognized by "transversalité" and "integration." We recognize the "transversalité" as an opportunity for the paradox and recognize the paradox itself when thinking about how to mitigate and overcome it. And "control" is used here to imply regulation and support. Additionally, "control" is also essentially interpreted as a purposive concept and is considered to be working when the conditions required to achieve a given goal are controlled.

Subsequently, this chapter explores the ways in which this business model can be used as processes and tools to regulate and support (that is, to control) the board of directors, an organ responsible for governance.[1]

Thus, first, Section 2.1 outlines recent trends in reform of board of directors by examining three reports to review its significance. Section 2.2 considers the aspects of the same examined by these reports and identifies how the reports build their argument. This section concludes that the debate on reform, as aforementioned, offers a perspective on "managing governance" through an active "offensive governance" approach rather than defensive approaches focused on preventing corporate misconduct. It also confirms that this approach and my idea of governance control have similar orientations.

Based on this discussion, Section 3 uses the theory of control to approach governance. Section 3.1 considers the significance of controlling the board of directors, which is responsible for governance. If this type of control constitutes "governance control," the subject of control would be the board of directors. Section 3.2 employs the idea of paradox in the French theory of control as the conceptual basis to examine the use of a business model expected to effectively control governance. Finally, this chapter concludes with a summary of the entire argument.

---

[1] This chapter relies on Bouquin (1991) for the definition of management control (p. 35): "A process and system that ensures that the manager, thanks to operation control, will achieve or has achieved a consistency between strategic choices and current actions." Additionally, management accounting is briefly defined as "one of the models of monetary flows." This chapter is a revised version of the article published in the magazine *Sangyo Keiri*.

2. Recent Trends in Reform of Board of Directors

2.1 *Significance of Double Codes and Ito Review*

"Double Codes" here refer to the Corporate Governance Code implemented in June 2015 and the Stewardship Code already administered since February 2014. The Financial Services Agency primarily promoted the Double Codes. Along with the amendment to the Companies Act that took place around the same time, the Double Codes constitute new trends in corporate governance reform.

Introduction in the *Corporate Governance Code Draft* by the Expert Committee on Formulating the Corporate Governance Code (Tokyo Stock Exchange, 2015) summarizes the significance of the Code in the following way. The Code (draft) aims at realizing "offensive governance" by ensuring transparency and fairness in corporate decision-making. This includes accountability to stakeholders in terms of obligations while promoting swift and bold decision-making based on the said attributes. Rather than overly emphasizing the avoidance or mitigation of risks at companies and the prevention of misconduct, the Code attempts to realize such "offensive governance" primarily by promoting the exercise of healthy entrepreneurship and facilitating sustainable corporate growth and mid- and long-term improvements in corporate value.[2]

Corporate governance is defined in the main body of the Corporate Governance Code as follows: "Corporate governance refers to a system in which companies exercise transparent/fair and swift/bold decision-making by taking into account the circumstances of shareholders, customers, employees, local communities, and so forth (Tokyo Stock Exchange, 2015, p. 2)." It seeks to contribute to the development of companies,

---

[2]Expert Committee on Formulating the Corporate Governance Code (2015), *Introduction* in *Corporate Governance Code Draft*. As a side note, this Corporate Governance Code (Japan Edition) was first formulated by the Expert Committee on Formulating the Corporate Governance Code, which was jointly established by the Financial Services Agency and the Tokyo Stock Exchange, and then it was incorporated into the regulations for the listing of securities by individual stock exchanges. Therefore, the correct reference would be Tokyo Stock Exchange, Inc. (2015), *Japan's Corporate Governance Code: Seeking Sustainable Corporate Growth and Increased Corporate Value over the Mid- to Long-Term*. Watanabe (2015) was used to understand this history.

investors, and, eventually, the entire economy by encouraging each company to autonomously formulate strategies for sustainable growth and the mid- and long-term improvement in corporate value through proper exercise of corporate governance.

The Corporate Governance Code seeks to realize such "offensive governance" by setting forth five basic principles: (1) securing the rights and equal treatment of shareholders, (2) appropriate cooperation with stakeholders other than shareholders, (3) ensuring appropriate information disclosure and transparency, (4) responsibilities of the board, and (5) dialog with shareholders. Instead of a detailed analysis of each of these principles, we specifically focused on the fourth principle and examined it in greater detail to explore recent trends in the board of directors' reform.

Summary of the fourth principle is as follows:

The board of directors of listed companies should, based on its fiduciary responsibility and accountability to shareholders, promote the company's sustainable growth and mid- and long-term improvement in corporate value and enhance earnings power and capital efficiency by properly fulfilling its roles and obligations including (1) setting the broad direction of corporate strategy, (2) establishing an environment where appropriate risk-taking by the senior management is supported, and (3) effectively overseeing directors and management (including the executive officer and the so-called corporate officers) from an independent and objective standpoint (p. 4).

This principle essentially describes the need for the board of directors to formulate corporate strategies, provide general directions to the executive officer and directors, facilitate the development of an environment where they can exercise risk-taking, and oversee these individuals. The configuration suggested here is the same as, for example, the "governance-based management" proposed by Toyama and Sawa (2015). Both models expect the board of directors to play the role of a "monitoring board." This is discussed later.

The following section examines "expectations for how the board of directors is supposed to be" to organize the board of directors' role expectations. However, prior to this, we briefly discuss the other code,

Stewardship Code (The Council of Experts on the Stewardship Code) (Japan Edition, 2014), and offer some comments on the relationship between Double Codes and *Ito Review*.

The seven principles of the Stewardship Code can be summarized as follows: Determining and making guidelines available for fulfilling stewardship responsibilities, understanding conditions of the invested companies, engaging in purposeful dialog, and making efforts toward common understanding; building a clear vision regarding the exercise of voting rights and connecting them to the sustainable growth of invested companies, and regularly reporting how stewardship responsibilities are being fulfilled (p. 6).

This summary essentially describes how institutional investors are supposed to be. The Stewardship Code demands that the responsibilities of institutional investors and expected roles of the board of trustees work together in an integrated manner. That is, institutional investors and invested companies are expected to engage in purposeful dialog.[3]

Finally, we discuss the relationship between Double Codes and *Ito Review* (implemented since August 2014). The argument in the *Ito Review*, which has been promoted by the Ministry of Economy, Trade and Industry, is not significantly different from those underscoring the Double Codes. The *Ito Review* formulates a model of corporate governance reform that links the reform in governance function of the board of directors within the realm of corporate management and the stewardship responsibilities of institutional investors. The *Ito Review* problematizes issues based on the perception that there is something wrong with the fact that an innovative country like Japan is tolerating sustained low profitability.

---

[3] It is useful to mention two additional approaches unique to the Stewardship Code. One is the principle-based approach, and the other one is the principle of *Comply or Explain*. The first is not a rule-based approach that specifies, in detail, the actions institutional investors are supposed to take. Instead, this code sets forth a principle-based approach wherein it is assumed that the implementation of the code is left for individual institutional investors who would creatively apply it according to their specific circumstance. Additionally, *Comply or Explain* refers to an approach wherein companies are expected to either implement the principles in the Code or explain why they decided not to implement them.

In short, the analysis in the *Ito Review* suggests that in the period after the 1990s, the "double-standard management" (a type of management that was practiced until the 1980s when Japanese companies were doing well in which many Japanese companies promised profitability to the short-term-oriented capital market while managing companies from a long-term perspective), among other factors, caused the absence or weakening of interests in capital efficiency and improvement in corporate value. It then suggests countering this by discontinuing customs and legacy practices that could hinder sustainable growth and by facilitating sustainable value creation through "co-creation" between companies and investors. As the *Ito Review*'s subtitle states, it advocates cultivating favorable relationships between companies and investors.

So far, we briefly highlighted the respective significance of the Double Codes and *Ito Review*. The fundamental argument therein is precisely what we stated at the beginning of this chapter. That is, their argument is closely linked to the fact that the focus of recent debate on corporate governance is witnessing a shift from defensive aspects to "offensive governance." Each report, speaking from its specific standpoint, repeatedly called for the need to make creative efforts to build desirable relationships between companies and investors. The board of directors in charge of the company's governance are increasingly expected to play the key role in ensuring that such requests are fulfilled. These reports argue that the board of directors is currently the only entity capable of performing this task in a reliable and steady manner. These points have commonalities with the analytical framework of "controlling the governance" addressed in this chapter.

Since then, the above Double Codes have been revised twice in 2018 and 2021. In particular, the 2021 revision has been made to address the spread of new coronavirus infections (COVID-19) and recent climate change (Tokyo Stock Exchange, 2021). Therefore, the main issue of the revision is to tackle sustainability issues, although it claims to further strengthen the functions surrounding the appointment of independent outside directors. In particular, it can be said that it is limited to the disclosure of climate change based on the framework of the Task Force on Climate-Related Financial Disclosure (TCFD).

2.2 *Expectations for how the board of directors is supposed to be: Perspectives of Business Law, Management Studies, and Enterprise Risk Management (ERM)*

Based on the analysis so far, the "expectations for how the board of directors is supposed to be" can be understood by paying greater attention to the role the board of directors plays as a "monitoring board," which we discuss later.

As aforementioned regarding principle 4 of the Corporate Governance Code, the board of directors is required to improve the company's sustainable growth and mid- and long-term corporate values as well as enhance earnings power and capital efficiency. To reiterate, the board of directors must provide general directions, such as corporate strategies, facilitate the development of an environment where corporate officers can exercise risk-taking, and oversee these individuals. This aligns perfectly with "governance-based management" proposed by Toyama and Sawa (2015). It refers to the role of the board of directors as a "monitoring board."

Figure 1 compares two types of board of directors. We can understand the components of "governance-based management" proposed by Toyama and Sawa (2015).

	Management-Based Board	Monitoring-Based Board
Current situation	Many Japanese companies have so far had this model	The role model played by directors, especially those played by independent outside directors.
Primary role of the board	Conduct individual business operations	The *ex-post* supervision carried out by independent outside directors on the entire business operation.
Characters of decision-making	Higher level of specialization and slower speed. Unsuitable for drastic decision-making that leaves no room for ambiguity or decision-making that is less compatible with organizational harmony.	This type of board also practices drastic decision-making with no scope for ambiguity. Other types of less important decision-making are relegated to the company president and other corporate officers.
Governance function	The Board will not be able to exercise its governance function.	Powerful if independent outside directors function.

Figure 1. Comparison of Management-Based and Monitoring-Based Boards

Source: Toyama and Sawa (2015, p. 113).

The two types refer to the management-based board and the monitoring-based board. Many Japanese companies have so far had a board of directors in which the board members are co-appointed as corporate officers. Thus, given that the primary role of the board is to conduct individual business operations, we can classify this type of board as a management-based board. As shown in Figure 1, the decision-making in the management-based board is characterized by a higher level of specialization and slower speed. Further, this type of board is unsuitable for drastic decision-making that leaves no room for ambiguity or decision-making that is less compatible with organizational harmony. Therefore, the board will not be able to exercise its governance function.

In contrast, the monitoring-based board relies primarily on the role played by directors, especially those played by independent outside directors. The primary feature of this type of board is the *ex post* supervision carried out by independent outside directors on the entire business operation. This type of board also practices drastic decision-making with no scope for ambiguity. Other types of less important decision-making are relegated to the company president and other corporate officers. These features enable decision-making that is not only swift but also grounded in specialized business operations.

In "governance-based management" proposed by Toyama and Sawa (2015), "when governance is working," it means that "the exertion of power is functioning properly in the organization (Toyama and Sawa, 2015, p. 118)." The following extended quote highlights vital points regarding the following:

It is required for a monitoring-based board of directors to recognize the appointment of the president as its paramount and ultimate mission and to lead long-term sustainable growth of the company. In both the Kanebo and Toshiba cases, the greatest fault in governance was that the board not only continued to appoint corporate officers who postponed making hard decisions — selecting options to pursue and getting rid of all other options — but also failed to remove corporate officers who continued to give impossible orders that would lead to accounting fraud. The flip side of this is that because the board has a significant responsibility regarding the exercise of the right to remove the president, independent outside directors, whether their opinions are supported by the majority of the board or not, are expected to have spirit and commitment to challenge the board by being always ready to exercise the powerful right to enter a motion to dismiss the president when necessary (Toyama and Sawa, 2015, pp. 118–119).

Clearly, at the heart of this argument lies the right of the board to dismiss corporate managers. This right enables a monitoring-based board to exercise its greatest and the most important role.

This discussion was from the broad perspective of Business Law. Corporate governance can also be questioned from the standpoint of Management Studies. Uchida (2013) accurately organized existing literature on corporate governance and classified research approaches for board of directors into controlled and collaborative approaches, as shown in Figure 2.

The relationship between the management and board of directors is further classified into the control approach derived from economics and the collaborative approach derived from sociology (for details of the analysis, see Uchida (2013)). Unfortunately, there is a lack of further analysis on governance of control beyond this classification.

We discussed the importance of an institutional setting based on the monitoring-based board derived from Business Law by focusing on the

Controlled Approach		**Collaborative Approach**
Agency theory (economics/finance)	Theoretical bases	Stewardship theory (sociology/psychology)
Economic human (selfish/ opportunistic, extrinsic)	Management assumptions (human model, behavioral characteristics, motives)	Self-actualizing human beings (collective/organizational representative, endogenous)
Conflict relationship	Relationship between management and the board of directors	Collaborative relationship
Maximize principal profits: resolve conflicts of interest	Control system	Maximize organizational profits Delegation of authority
Management supervision Incentive design	Board function	Support for management Providing human and social capital

Figure 2.   Controlled Approach and Collaborative Approach

Source: Uchida (2013, p. 95).

details of "governance-based management" proposed by Toyama and Sawa (2015). Following this, we briefly reviewed how Management Studies articulated our issues.

The central discussion in both cases is limited to institutional design, such as the board of directors, or aspects related to the personality and characteristics of corporate managers. Why are we limiting our discussion only to institutional design for promoting governance instead of extending it to the nature of "management" in governance and "controlling governance" which I suggest? Does this indicate that governance-based management can be achieved only by establishing a monitoring-based board of directors through institutional design? Focusing on the latter, this chapter raises a question: Why do we not control governance?

It must be noted that the concept of governance control I propose is not merely a subjective idea. I would like to reiterate that this concept was originally developed through elaborate analysis of four hypotheses generated as outcomes in my own research on French managerial accounting and theories of management control (Oshita, 2009).

Of these four hypotheses, the fourth one posited that "the debate on internal control triggered by corporate misconduct and accounting fraud prompts us to consider strategies to control governance (leading to the concept of governance control)." To generate the concept of governance control stated in this hypothesis, I examined French managerial accounting and theories of management control for an extended period.

As addressed in the following section, using Henri Bouquin's managerial control theory more recently as an inspiration revealed one aspect of the mechanism wherein strategies and management control are linked to each other through a unique business model. That is, focus on a business model that incorporates a mechanism to mitigate paradoxes of control showed that this business model would help us conceptualize the governance control I envisioned. I employed this business model as a base to identify the elevated urgency of the concept of governance control. For this, I considered the issues raised by corporate internal systems, including COSO's "Internal Control" (COSO, 1992) and ERM (COSO, 2004), which expanded and incorporated internal control. These systems were developed in response to corporate misconduct and accounting fraud. Although details cannot be discussed here due to the limited space, the 2017 issue of COSO (ERM) is also an innovative report that argues the importance of the idea of governance in enterprise risk management (COSO, 2017). These COSO reports are closely related to the fact that recent debates on corporate governance highlight negative aspects, such as the prevention of misconduct as well as, more importantly, the "offensive governance" approach.

So far, this chapter focused on the urgency of controlling governance, which is uniformly missing in Business Law, Management Studies, and COSO's ERM, and it called for the importance of the role of "controlling the governance," which regulates and supports organs, especially the board of directors responsible for governance.

The following section examines the processes and tools for controlling the governance of the board of directors.

3. Approaching Governance Using the Theory of Control

3.1 *Controlling the board of directors responsible for governance*

The previous section highlighted the aspect of "managing governance." This is precisely the direction that corporate governance reform must follow based on reform of board of directors. This chapter addresses "controlling the governance" from the standpoint of the theory of corporate control, which uses an approach that differs from the existing debate on reform of board of directors.

Figure 3 depicts three sets of three-layer structures concerning control/audit. These three sets of control/audit are isomorphic as they all have a

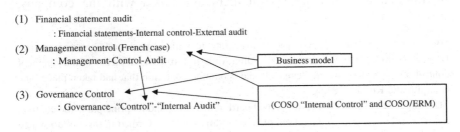

(1) Financial statement audit
    : Financial statements-Internal control-External audit
(2) Management control (French case)
    : Management-Control-Audit   Business model
(3) Governance Control
    : Governance- "Control"-"Internal Audit"   (COSO "Internal Control" and COSO/ERM)

Figure 3.   Three Sets of Three-Layer Structures for Control/Audit

three-layer structure. Control, always accompanied by audit, is directed toward individual targets. Figure 3 shows how the business model addressed in this chapter is utilized in respective forms of control: management control (2) and governance control (3). In the former, this business model serves as a guide when linking formulated strategies to management control. In the case of the latter, the business model is expected to be used for regulating and supporting governance, particularly that of the board of directors, while formulating strategies (within the context of strategic control) prior to management control.[4]

To state the conclusion, if the business model is utilized in these ways, governance control would help the board of directors create value based on value-added calculation, formulate an economic model for value allocation, and create a mechanism for collaboration within and outside the company through the formulation of such a model.[5] The following section identifies the structure and function of the model for value-added calculation, which can be understood as a tool for governance control.

3.2 *Using a business model that is effective for governance control*

One of the effective tools for governance control proposed in this chapter is likely to be Bouquin's business model. Its structure and function are discussed in the following to the extent befitting our discussion.

The following are the characteristics of this business model (Figure 4). First, this model has a structure for computing value-added calculations. Starting with where, how, and how much customer value is generated, the model describes how value creation and value allocation are carried out by internal and external stakeholders associated with the company,

---

[4] Bouquin's three systems of control refer to strategic, management, and operation control. Bouquin formulated these systems expanding Anthony's traditional theory of management control by incorporating the changes in the economic condition that had taken place. See Bouquin and Kuszla (2013).

[5] The target of governance control is the board of directors, and its principal is the controller. It is still unclear as to what kind of relationship would be formed in this circumstance between the governance controller and the controller, which is principal in management control. We need to continue investigating this question in the future.

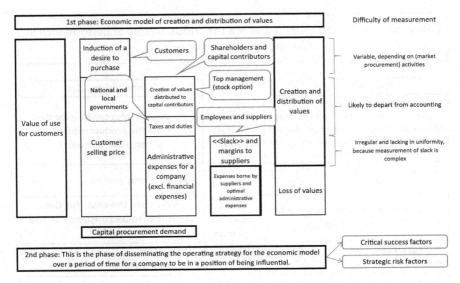

Figure 4. Business Model As a Coordinate Axis for Management Control

Source: Bouquin and Kuszla (2013, p. 50).

including customers, shareholders/providers of capital (creditors), top management, government offices, and employees/contractors. Naturally, cost components incurred by contractors and components for management optimization (unavoidable cost components) are excluded from the value creation component, and they are designated as value lost. This first state is explained as an economic model for value creation and value allocation.

The economic model from the first stage is implemented in the second stage. Briefly, it is a mechanism to let the strategies formulated as an economic model in the first stage diffuse downward in the second stage. In this mechanism, the distinctive feature of the model is to diffuse strategies in the management control stage in terms of both positive aspects — success factors — and negative aspects — risk factors. Figure 5 outlines the process of this downward diffusion.

Figure 5 shows a mechanism in which value-creation and allocation strategies are incorporated into the Strategic (supply, process, and resources) and Financial models (sales, cost, and investment) in terms of key success and strategic risk factors. The earlier Strategic and Financial

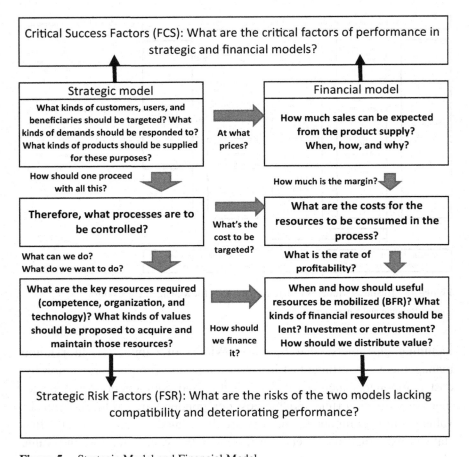

Figure 5. Strategic Model and Financial Model

Source: Bouquin and Kuszla (2013, p. 80). The title is by the author.

models are sandwiched between key success factors (KSF) from the top and strategic risk factors (SRF) from the bottom. It is also important to note that the Strategic model is expressed with non-financial indicators and the Financial model with financial indicators.

Additionally, we should also acknowledge that the concept of paradox in control is incorporated in these two models. That is, each of the two models has a three-layer structure where the first layer is "supply/sales," the second layer is "process/cost," and the third layer is "resources/investment," and these layers correspond to competitiveness, value creation, and sustainability. From the very outset, Bouquin recognizes paradoxes between competitiveness, value creation, and sustainability in the two models' three-layer structure representing the basic structure of corporate management.

Thus, both the Strategic and Financial models exercise control in "success key factors (FCS)" and "strategic risk factors (FSR)" by sandwiching the models using key factors (FCS) from the top and strategic risk factors (FSR) from the bottom, incorporating the three developmental stages of management accounting and control. From this point on, the familiar process of management control takes off.

This section approached governance by employing the theory of control. We then considered a business model suggested by Henri Bouquin as a practical tool for controlling the board of directors principally responsible for governance. At the base of this model is the mechanism for value-added calculation, which is the basic structure of this business model. When the use of this business model in the strategy formulation stage is grounded in the mechanism of value-added calculation, the model can facilitate more collaboration among a greater number of internal and external stakeholders.

In connection with the above discussion, it should be noted that British sociologist Ronald Dore was already making an interesting proposal early on in the corporate governance debate. In fact, Dore had the vision to create and implement a value-added calculation sheet at the governance level utilizing the principle of value-added calculation, which serves as the foundation of Bouquin's business model. According to Dore, this value-added calculation sheet is a method to instill in corporate managers an awareness that is appropriate for stakeholder companies. The sheet reveals the value that has been collectively created by the knowledge and physical labor of managers, engineers, and office and production workers using capital received from shareholders and banks. Dore proposed this calculation sheet based on this understanding (Dore, 2006).

As already discussed, many recent propositions concerning corporate governance, including the Double Codes, primarily focus on how the board of directors is supposed to be as a corporate organ and the dialog between companies and investors. However, these propositions do not offer any discussion regarding the forms of control that can regulate and support the board of directors.

However, in 2019, the TCFD Consortium mentioned above announced the "Climate Change-Related Information Utilization Guidance for Promoting Green Investment" (TCFD Consortium, 2020). There, a logical structure reminiscent of Bouquin's control theory can be seen as a perspective that investors should understand in line with TCDF's recommendations. That is, governance, strategies and business models, risks, and opportunities are followed by performance and key performance indicators (KPIs). If we consider KPIs to correspond to FCS and FRS in Figure 5, we can understand the similarities between them. In that sense, it can be confirmed here that it is necessary to steadily integrate internal governance and external governance while aiming for a virtuous cycle of environment and growth, triggered by the recognition of the climate change crisis.

This chapter is a small attempt to clarify the current situation in order to explain the necessity of control at the governance level.[6] It hopefully raises a meaningful question from the perspective of the theory of control in debates regarding corporate governance reform.

4. Conclusion

Until the 1980s, when Japanese companies were doing well, it was possible to promise profitability to the short-term-oriented capital market on one hand while practicing management from a long-term perspective and making long-term investment toward innovation on the other hand. However, the *Ito Review* understood that when the profitability of Japanese companies declined since the 1990s as the Japanese economy experienced globalization amidst the collapse of the bubble economy, it was debunked that companies, while communicating interests in prioritizing return on equity (ROE) and other indicators emphasized by that capital market, internally prioritized other indicators that adhered to the company's internal logic.

Especially since the 2000s, as the Japanese economy became more globalized and the presence of overseas investors grew, we began observing a strong tendency whereby companies increased dividends for

---

[6] For example, Takayama's (2014) attempt on "Board Evaluation" is likely to suggest an aspect of the nature of governance control regulating and supporting the board of directors.

shareholders and executive compensation while reducing the allocation for salaries and capital investment. Owing to prioritizing immediate gains, companies failed to update obsolete facilities. Consequently, these obsolete facilities had to handle voluminous orders that exceeded their production capacity, straining production sites. Thus, there has been a significant amount of media coverage recently on fraudulent quality control on production sites. Many of these cases involved falsification of data to meet the delivery date. These instances of misconduct or fraud in production sites do not seem to stop (Horigome, 2018).

The cause of these fraudulent incidents on production sites can now be traced not only to the managerial level but also, and more frequently, to the governance level.[7] To highlight the issue with management policy where companies increase dividends for shareholders as the presence of overseas investors becomes more prominent while reducing salaries and capital investment, there is now a strong demand for the promotion of sustainable growth through dialog with shareholders as correctly suggested in the Double Codes and the creation of mid- and long-term corporate values. We now see the potential to reduce fraud to a certain extent by practicing such activities. In this regard, this chapter sets great expectations for governance-level control.

By focusing on the board of directors, which is the primary body responsible for governance, this chapter tentatively shows a framework for regulating and supporting the board of directors. As stated repeatedly, if the business model is utilized in these ways, governance control would help the board of directors create value based on value-added calculation, formulate an economic model for value allocation, and create a mechanism for collaboration within and outside the company through formulating such a model. This is where the question raised in this chapter originated from: Why do we not control governance? However, we still have not fully identified the details of controlling governance. Thus, this question requires continued investigation investigation in the future.

---

[7]Additionally, Shishido's (2017) view to analyze the monitoring board from the perspective of the complementary relationship between internal governance and external governance also encourages us to examine the relationship between management and governance control.

Acknowledgments

I would like to express my sincere gratitude to the faculty staff and administrative staff of Shimonoseki City University for their tremendous support in the preparation of this paper. In addition, this paper is part of the research results of the 2022 Grant-in-Aid for Scientific Research (C) of the Japan Society for the Promotion of Science.

References

Bouquin, H. (1991). *Le Contrôle de gestion*, 2nd ed., PUF, Paris.

Bouquin, H. and Kuszla, C. (2013). *Le Contrôle de gestion*, 10th ed., PUF, Paris.

Committee of Sponsoring Organizations of the Treadway Commission (COSO). (2017). *Enterprise Risk Management: Integrating with Strategy and Performance*, AICPA.

Committee of Sponsoring Organizations of the Treadway Commission (COSO). (1992). *Internal Control-Integrated Framework*, AICPA.

Committee of Sponsoring Organizations of the Treadway Commission (COSO). (2004). *Enterprise Risk Management-Integrated Framework*, AICPA.

Dore, D. (2006). *Who Should the Company Be for*, Iwanami Shoten, Tokyo (in Japanese).

Horigome, T. (2018). *Injustice in the Manufacturing Industry, From Eliminating the Stuffiness of the Site*, Asahi Shimbun, Tokyo (in Japanese).

Ito Review (2014). *Competitiveness and Incentives for Sustainable Growth — Building Desirable Relationships between Companies and Investors*, Project Final Report (in Japanese).

Japanese Stewardship Code Experts Study Group (2014). *Principles of Responsible Institutional Investors Japanese Stewardship Code — To Promote Sustainable Growth of Companies through Investment and Dialogue* (in Japanese).

Oshita, J. (2009). *Modern French Management Accounting — Accounting, Control, Governance*, Chuokeizai-sha, Tokyo (in Japanese).

Shishido, Z. (2017). Rethinking the Monitoring Board — From the Viewpoint of Complementarity of Internal Governance and External Governance (Kuronuma, E. and Fujita, T. (2017). *Course of Corporate Law (Kenjiro Egashira Memorial)*, Yuhikaku Publishing, Tokyo), pp. 231–262 (in Japanese).

Takayama, Y. (2014). Board Evaluation and Corporate Governance: From Form to Effectiveness, *Shoji Homu* (Commercial Legal Affairs), No. 2043, pp. 15–26 (in Japanese).

TCFD Consortium (2020). *Guidance 2.0 on Climate-related Financial Information Disclosures*, (in Japanese). https://tcfd-consortium.jp/pdf/news/20073103/TCFD%20Guidance%202_0_2.pdf (last access on 2023.2.4).

Tokyo Stock Exchange (2015). *Corporate Governance Code-For Sustainable Growth of the Company and Improvement of Corporate Value over the Medium to Long Term-*, (in Japanese). https://www.fsa.go.jp/en/refer/councils/corporategovernance/20150306-1/01.pdf (last access on 2023.2.4).

Tokyo Stock Exchange (2021). *Corporate Governance Code-For Sustainable Growth of the Company and Improvement of Corporate Value over the Medium to Long Term* (in Japanese). https://www.fsa.go.jp/en/news/2021/20210611/06.pdf (last access on 2023.2.4).

Toyama, K. and Sawa, Y. (2015). *This Is Governance Management*, Tokyo Keizai Inc, Tokyo (in Japanese).

Uchida, D. (2013). Toward Corporate Governance in the Growth Period — Review of Existing Research and Future Issues, *Frontier of Japanese Corporate Research*, No. 9, edited by Hitotsubashi University Japanese Corporate Research Center, pp. 90–102 (in Japanese).

Watanabe, S. (2015). Understanding the Corporate Governance Code, *Shoji Homu* (Commercial Legal Affairs), Tokyo (in Japanese).

Chapter 3

The Function of Top Management in This Age of Sustainability

Kazuyoshi Morimoto

Hagoromo University of International Studies
Osaka, Japan

1. Introduction

Morimoto (2019) analyzed the congruence between the top management's goals and divisional managers' performance goals using the theory of agency relationships. The top management, who is required to enhance shareholders' value, acts as a principal and controls the divisional managers who act as agents trying to pursue the organizational goals of the decentralized units. From the mathematical equality of both a valuation method based on free cash flows (FCF method) and another on residual income (RI method), the value of a firm to its shareholders increases when divisional managers try to increase the periodical amount of its residual income. Thus, Morimoto (2019) concluded that the system of selecting residual income as a divisional manager's performance measure and devising an incentive scheme based on this measure was most suitable for achieving goal congruence between the top management and divisional managers to maximize shareholders' value.

However, after going through the book, *The Moral Economy* by Bowles, I began questioning the agency model that emphasized on providing economic and monetary incentives. Bowles (2016) insists that fines, rewards, and other material inducements often do not work well, and incentives alone cannot provide the foundations of good governance. According to Bowles (2016), the greater use of monetary incentives to guide individual behavior promotes self-interest so that ethical and other-regarding motivations essential for good governance may be undermined by excessive incentives of this kind. Consequently, Bowles (2016) wishes to advance the policy paradigm of synergy between economic incentives and other-regarding motivations (Bowles, 2016, p. 7).

Morimoto (2019) studied the principal-agent relationship in the Japanese automobile industry from the viewpoint of the moral economy emphasized by Bowles (2016). In this agency relationship, the automaker acts as a principal and the parts manufacturers act as agents. As has been widely discussed, automakers in Japan have maintained longstanding transactional relations with parts manufacturers and established collaborative and reciprocal relations in the form of keiretsu alignments. The automaker absorbs the risks that the parts manufacturers ought to bear and collaborates with them to create joint margins. Moreover, the joint margin is allocated fairly between both parties. Therefore, Morimoto (2019) concluded that the principal–agent relationship in the Japanese automobile industry is a contractual relationship in which both the maintenance of economic rationality through profit acquisition and the maintenance of equality through profit sharing can be achieved simultaneously. The author believes that the practices in the Japanese automobile industry after the oil shocks of the 1970s can be the subject of research on today's sustainable management.

A firm's sustainability is assured by considering profit, people, and planet (Monden, 2017, p. 87). In today's sustainability-rich business environment, firms are expected to earn economic profits in ways that benefit the society and protect the planet. Thus, a firm's top management ought to create profitable solutions to address the problems of the people and the planet. About 45 years ago, with the recognition of environmental regulations, demands for labor union participation in management decision-making bodies, demands for improving working conditions, and growing movements for consumer protection, Monden (1978) stated the following, remarkable argument: "Therefore, today's enterprises must meet profits goals and other goals at the same time. Thus, how to adjust the conflicts among such multi-goals is a realistic problem of modern enterprises

(Monden, 1978, p. 4)." While keeping in mind Monden's (1978) question, this study explores sustainable management in the case where the top management pursues mediation of conflicts among multiple goals. This study aims to show that the top management plays the roles in converting the conflicts among multiple goals into constructive cooperation and mediating the interests of all parties involved in sustainable management.

2. Control and Empowerment

Following the framework of agency theory, Morimoto (2019) endeavored to address agency problems between the top management and divisional managers. Jensen and Meckling (1976), proponents of the agency theory, define an agency relationship as a contract under which principals engage an agent to perform some service on behalf of them. In agency relationships, both the principals and agents seek to maximize their own utility rationally. Jensen and Meckling (1976) also mention that the relationship between the shareholders and the manager of a corporation fits the definition of a pure agency relationship. According to them, a manager is a utility maximizer and may not always take actions that are in the best interests of the shareholders. A conflict of interest always exists between the shareholders and managers. Jensen and Meckling (1976) suggest methods in which shareholders as principles control managers' behaviors as agents through monitoring. These monitoring methods include auditing, formal control systems, budget restrictions, and the establishment of incentive compensation systems (Jensen and Meckling, 1976, p. 323).

Stewardship theory is an alternative approach to agency theory. Donaldson and Davis (1991) and Davis *et al.* (1997) argue that stewardship theory has roots in psychology and sociology. Stewardship theorists do not use the term agents; they refer to the agents as stewards and analyze the relationship between the shareholders and top executives as a principal–steward relationship. According to the stewardship theory, the stewards will not substitute self-serving behaviors for cooperative behaviors because they place higher value on cooperation than on self-seeking behaviors (Davis *et al.*, 1997, p. 24). Stewards want to do a good job, and ensure their growth, achievement, and self-actualization through accomplishing organizational objectives rather than personal objectives. Thus, monitoring and other control activities for stewards lower their motivation and can potentially be counterproductive. The stewardship theorists aim at structural situations in which executives are motivated to behave in the best interests of their principals. Davis *et al.* (1997) conclude that empowering governance structures are more appropriate than controlling governance structures if the executives' motivations fit the model of man underlying stewardship theory (Davis *et al.*, 1997, p. 25).

Donaldson and Davis (1991) examined the empirical validity of the agency and stewardship theories with respect to the role and reward of chief executive officer (CEO). According to them, agency theorists require the separation of roles of the chair and CEO to safeguard returns to shareholders; however, the stewardship theorists seek to make empowering structural situations by combining the roles of the chair and CEO. The structure of a corporate board, in which the CEO is also the chair of the board of directors, is termed CEO duality. Donaldson and Davis (1991) stress that their study primarily focuses on the role structure issue of CEO duality rather than on the issue of rewards. They also frame two hypotheses each for both the agency theory and the stewardship theory regarding CEO duality and CEO rewards. The stewardship theory yields two opposing hypotheses to the two hypotheses that the agency theory yields. Donaldson and Davis (1991), after testing the four hypotheses, concluded that the empirical tests' results fail to support the agency theory but provide some support to the stewardship theory. Their empirical evidence explains that returns to shareholders are improved by combining the roles of the chair and the CEO. Thus, empowering governance structures where the CEO is also the chair of the board helps the CEO attain superior performance by taking autonomous actions because the CEO as a steward exercises complete authority over the corporation (Donaldson and Davis, 1991, p. 62). However, the risk-averse shareholders prefer agency governance prescriptions to stewardship governance prescriptions because they believe that their interests can be safeguarded only by using the control checks and incentive compensation schemes to motivate the CEO. The prescriptions of the agency theory can be viewed as necessary costs for protecting shareholders' interests against the risks of an opportunistic shirker (Davis *et al.*, 1997, p. 26).

As previously mentioned, stewardship theorists do not focus on placing the management under shareholder controls but on empowering the management to take autonomous executive actions. The essential points of learning from stewardship theorists are as follows: First, the motivation of man is not the pursuit of money or utility but the creation of worthwhile endeavors or self-actualization. Second, organizational members' good performance is created by self-governing arrangements rather than monitoring and controlling. Third, returns to shareholders are improved by the cooperative behaviors of the stewards whose behaviors derive from their other-regarding motivations. Thus, the stewardship theorists provide useful suggestions for building sustainable management where the top management seeks to profitably solve the problems of the people, organization, and society.

3. Roles and Responsibilities of the Board of Directors

3.1 *Corporate governance codes*

The top management must incorporate the concept of sustainability into its management philosophy to ensure sustainable management. A management philosophy based on sustainability forms the foundation of organizational decision-making. Integration of sustainability into the organizational culture and operations of a firm is possible through its corporate credo and motto. The top management must build a sustainability-based planning process to help translate sustainability into specific performance targets for organizational members.

Many researchers emphasize the roles and responsibilities of the board of directors to achieve improved sustainability performance. For example, Elkington (1997), a proponent of the triple bottom line concept that focuses on economic prosperity, environmental quality, and social justice, says the following: "The sustainability agenda will often overlap the corporate governance agenda. High-performance boards are critical to the sustainability transition. More attention needs to be paid to the role of boards and directors in monitoring, understanding, prioritizing, and ensuring progress towards sustainability targets (Elkington, 1997, p. 300)."

According to Ito (2021), the board of directors is expected to play an important role in achieving sustainable corporate growth and capital efficiency. Moreover, Stead and Stead (2014), researchers of sustainable strategic management, suggest that the boards of directors must expand their responsibilities to include their firms' social, ecological, and economic performance when bringing sustainability to the boards. According to them, an appropriate board composition is key to establishing sustainable boards and building these boards will likely require adding directors representing non-shareholder interests, such as non-governmental organizations, citizen sector organizations, and labor unions (Stead and Stead, 2014, p. 235).

As an initiative to reform corporate governance to strengthen shareholder supremacy, the Stewardship Code and Corporate Governance Code have been introduced and revised in Japan (Miyajima and Saito, 2020). Japan's Corporate Governance Code was revised in June 2021; it was the second revision since its introduction in 2016. Further, the Guidelines for Investor and Company Engagement were revised in June 2021. The main revisions in Japan's Corporate Governance Code (2021) are as follows: (a) fulfilling the functions of the boards of directors, (b) ensuring diversity in the promotion of core human resources, and (c) dealing with sustainability issues. All the three points are related to the roles and responsibilities of the boards of directors.

With respect to (a) fulfilling the functions of the boards, Japan's Corporate Governance Code (2021) stresses that the boards of directors are responsible for governance functions owing to their fiduciary duties toward shareholders. These functions are as follows: (1) setting the broad direction for corporate strategy, (2) establishing an environment that supports appropriate risk-taking by senior management, and (3) carrying out effective supervision of the directors and management from an independent standpoint. According to Japan's Corporate Governance Code (2021), companies listed on the Prime Market should appoint at least one-third of their directors as independent directors. Other important guidelines by Japan's Corporate Governance Code (2021) are as follows: (1) monitoring the management through important decision-making by the board, including the appointment and dismissal of the senior management, (2) establishing independent nomination and remuneration committees under the board, (3) appointing the majority of the members of each committee as independent directors if a company is listed on the Prime Market, and (4) designing management remuneration systems that are linked to medium- or long-term results. Additionally, the Guidelines for Investor and Company Engagement (2021) necessitate the appointment of an independent director as the chairperson of the boards of directors.

For (b) ensuring diversity in the promotion of core human resources, and (c) dealing with sustainability issues, Japan's Corporate Governance Code (2021) emphasizes the roles and responsibilities of the boards of directors. The boards of directors should formulate a basic policy with the aim of promoting sustainable corporate growth and increasing corporate value over the medium to long term.

Japan's Corporate Governance Code (2021) provides the following five general principles: (1) securing the rights and equal treatment of shareholders, (2) appropriate cooperation with stakeholders other than shareholders, (3) ensuring appropriate information disclosure and transparency, (4) responsibilities of the board, and (5) dialog with shareholders. Although Japan's Corporate Governance Code (2021) sets a general principle on cooperation with stakeholders other than shareholders, it fundamentally follows the shareholder primacy model and recommends prescriptions for agency theory. The recommendations of prescriptions, such as monitoring, board composition, separation of the chair and CEO, remuneration systems, financial reporting, and investor relations, are all designed to safeguard shareholders' interests. From the perspective of sustainable management, the directors and senior management ought to run a company while serving the interests of not only the shareholders but also those of other stakeholders, such as employees, creditors, customers, suppliers, and the local community. The following section considers this.

3.2 Companies Act

To reform corporate governance, the Companies Act has been amended along with the introduction and revision of the Stewardship Code and the Corporate Governance Code. The principle of shareholders' profit maximization should be upheld in the Companies Act. According to Egashira

(2021), the principle of shareholders' profit maximization is the principle of mediating the interests of all parties involved in a stock company. That is because the owner of a firm is the residual claimant entitled to receive any net income that is left over after other stakeholders have been paid. Hence, the duties of loyalty imposed on directors and executive officers by Article 355 mean managerial obligations to maximize shareholder profits (Egashira, 2021, p. 23). According to Egashira (2021), however, the principle of shareholders' profit maximization is not ideal but is the next-best available solution. Therefore, the principle of shareholders' profit maximization must remain a loose principle with exceptions as a legal norm (Egashira, 2021, p. 25). Some of the exceptions set forth by Egashira (2021) are as follows:

(1) The provision of the articles of incorporation that substantially distribute a certain percentage of surplus to parties other than shareholders (social contribution, etc.) shall not be construed as invalid.

(2) Even if not stipulated in the articles of incorporation, it is not prohibited to run a company contrary to the maximization of shareholder profits with the agreement of all parties concerned.

(3) The demand for corporate social responsibility and corporate social contribution has been increasing in recent years, and the directors and executive officers have large discretion in this regard. Directors and executive officers may make donations that do not contribute to shareholders' interests.

(4) The directors and executive officers are given considerable discretion in making regular managerial decisions. Therefore, even if the directors and executive officers prioritize maintaining the employment of employees under the guise of maximizing the long-term returns of shareholders, it is often difficult for the shareholders to blame them for breaches of fiduciary duties.

In relation to the above-mentioned points, Tanaka (2021) argues that a company should be permitted to engage in social activities to a reasonable extent, even if this does not lead to the maximization of shareholder profits. For example, charitable activities such as donations to a reasonable extent, and management based on corporate social responsibility

(CSR) that serves the society and environment beyond what is required by the laws and regulations, do not violate the fiduciary duties of directors and executive officers, even if the profits of the company and shareholders are reduced (Tanaka, 2021, p. 274).

Tanaka (2020) also argues that it is not appropriate for the directors and executive officers to adhere to the shareholder primacy norm when conceiving externalities, such as pollution (Tanaka, 2020, pp. 83–85). The company should bear the costs of externalities such as pollution, even if it hampers shareholder profit maximization. Tanaka (2020) sets a 10% limit of shareholder profits that the directors and executive officers can sacrifice (Tanaka, 2020, p. 86).

As mentioned, the principle of shareholders' profit maximization should be upheld in the Companies Act. However, that principle is loose, with exceptions as a legal norm. According to the above jurists, therefore, directors and executive officers can include CSR in their management to a reasonable extent without being blamed for breaches of fiduciary duties. Thus, we can ensure that the Companies Act does not exclude CSR management. The following section considers the relationship between CSR and profits earned by a company.

4. Corporate Social Responsibility and Corporate Financial Performance

According to Tanimoto (2020), many empirical studies on the relationship between corporate social responsibility and financial performance have been conducted since the 1980s, mainly in the United States. Moreover, there are two ways to explain the relationship between CSR and financial performance: slack resources theory and good management theory (Tanimoto, 2020, p. 218). Following the works of McGuire *et al.* (1988) and Waddock and Graves (1997), this study examines the slack resource and good management theories.

McGuire *et al.* (1988) explored the relationship between CSR and financial performance using CSR data from *Fortune* magazine's survey of corporate reputations and financial performance data measured before and after 1983. They chiefly adopted two approaches in their work. First, they not only used accounting- and stock-market-based performance measures but also measures of risk. Second, they examined whether CSR predicts financial performance and vice versa.

The empirical results suggest the following conclusions (McGuire *et al.*, 1988, p. 868). First, CSR is more closely associated with prior financial performance than with subsequent financial performance. Second, financial performance measures tend to predict CSR better than risk does; however, measures of risk also explain a significant portion of the variability in CSR. Third, accounting-based performance measures, particularly return on assets (ROA), proved to be better predictors of CSR than stock-market-based performance measures. Firms with high performance and low risk may be better able to afford to act in a socially responsible manner (McGuire *et al.*, 1988, p. 869).

Waddock and Graves (1997) examined the empirical linkages between corporate social performance and financial performance in S&P 500 firms by using an improved source of data on corporate social performance. All companies in the S&P 500 are rated on multiple attributes considered relevant to corporate social performance. Five attributes of corporate social performance are considered more important than others as measures of social performance. They are community relations, employee relations, environment, product characteristics, and the treatment of women and minorities (Waddock and Graves, 1997, p. 307).

As noted above, McGuire *et al.* (1988) supported that prior high financial performance is generally a better predictor of CSR than subsequent performance is. Financially successful companies simply have more resources to spend in social domains, such as community relations, employee relations, and environment. Waddock and Graves (1997) argued that the empirical work of McGuire *et al.* (1988) supported the slack resource theory, in which better financial performance is a predictor of better corporate social performance. Waddock and Graves (1997) also characterized the view that better corporate social performance may lead to improved financial performance as good management theory. They empirically test whether there is a positive relationship between corporate social performance and financial performance and whether both slack resource and good management theories operate simultaneously.

They measured corporate financial performance using three accounting variables: return on assets (ROA), return on equity (ROE), and return on sales (ROS). First, they presented the results of the regression analysis using corporate social performance as the dependent variable and financial performance as the independent variable. Corporate social performance, as the dependent variable, is strongly related to ROA. When ROE and ROS were used as financial variables, the results were less strong but still significant. They found that corporate social performance is positively correlated with financial performance (Waddock and Graves, 1997, p. 310). Thus, they strongly supported the slack resource theory.

Further, they present the results of the regression analysis using financial performance variables, ROA, ROE, and ROS as the dependent variables, and corporate social performance as the independent variable (Waddock and Graves, 1997, p. 311). There is a significant relationship between ROA and corporate social performance and between ROS and corporate social performance. However, the relationship is not significant when ROE is used as a financial variable. Thus, they concluded that the results generally support the hypothesis of good management theory, in which financial performance depends on corporate social performance (Waddock and Graves, 1997, pp. 313–314).

Waddock and Graves (1997) supported both the slack resource and good management theories. The empirical works of McGuire *et al.* (1988) and Waddock and Graves (1997) ensure that there is a positive relationship between CSR and financial performance. Thus, we can expect the top management of a firm to include CSR in their management while seeking profitable solutions for the problems that the people and the planet face.

5. Corporation with Legal Personality

According to Mayer (2018), corporate laws create corporations, and a corporation is a legal fiction whose presence is defined, determined, and dependent on the corporate law (Mayer, 2018, p. 149). Jensen and Meckling (1976), agency theorists, recognize that the private corporations or firms are simply legal fictions that serve as a nexus for contracting relationships among individuals. Jensen and Meckling (1976), who view the firm as a nexus of contracts, argue that the personalization of the firm implied by asking questions such as "what should be the objective function of the firm" or "does the firm have a social responsibility" is seriously misleading. Although the firm is not an individual, we often make an error by considering the firms as persons with motivations and intentions (Jensen and Meckling, 1976, p. 311).

In contrast to Jensen and Meckling (1976), Mayer (2018) insists that the corporation is not a nexus of contracts but a nexus of relations between its constituent members based on trust, which depends on the commitment to the purpose of the corporation. The purpose of a corporation is not only to maximize shareholder value. The corporation is not a vehicle for controlling people involved in it for the benefit of a small class of privileged owners (Mayer, 2018, p. 222). It is a vehicle for committing to the fulfillment of its stated purposes (Mayer, 2018, p. 4). Mayer (2018) expects a board of trustees to make the vehicle work well. By creating a board of trustees, the owners of a corporation relinquish their rights to control and confer them to the board of directors responsible for increasing the value of the corporation (Mayer, 2018, p. 161). Thus, the board of directors has the responsibility of trustees to act on behalf of multiple parties.

According to Iwai (2009), a stock company consists of a dual ownership relationship in which the shareholders own the company as a legal person and the company as a legal person owns the company's assets. Moreover, a company as a legal person who sits in the middle of this dual ownership relationship plays the role of a person and a thing simultaneously. A corporation with a legal personality is not a mere private entity created by contracts between individuals but is essentially a public entity (Iwai, 2009, p. 99). In addition, the management of a stock company is not an agent of the shareholders but a trustee who has gained the confidence of the corporation (Iwai, 2009, p. 115). Thus, Iwai (2009), like Mayer (2018), suggests a contrasting view of the corporation from that of the agency theorists.

According to Iwai (2009), a corporate organization is a network of human assets that are specific to an organization. This organization-specific attribute of human assets gives rise to hold-up problems. When the asset is specific to a particular organization, the owner of the specific asset can be held up. When the employees, who are specific to serving the corporate organization, are threatened dismissal, they can be held up. The employees, fearing the possibility of future hold-ups, might not invest time and energy in brushing up their skills. According to Iwai (2009), the employees share the company's fate. The company, as a legal person, becomes the virtual owner of organization-specific human assets and protects its employees from hold-ups by external shareholders (Iwai, 2009, p. 193). A stock company with a dual ownership relationship can establish various organizational forms, such as a shareholder privilege company or a stakeholder participation company (Iwai, 2009, p. 299).

Finally, this section discusses the roles of the board of directors from the viewpoint of public corporation law. Blair and Stout (1999) argue that public corporation law encourages directors to serve the joint interests of all stakeholders who comprise the corporate team by insulating them from the demands of any single stakeholder group, including the shareholders. Directors are independent hierarchs charged not with serving shareholders' interests alone but with serving the interests of the legal entity known as the corporation (Blair and Stout, 1999, p. 288). Corporate directors owe their fiduciary duties to the corporation.

6. Conclusion

The purpose of this study is to show the function of top management in today's sustainability-rich business environment. It first took up the stewardship theory proposed in the 1990s and compared it with agency theories. Stewardship theorists did not focus on controlling management but on empowering management to take autonomous actions. It was found that superior performance of management could be achieved by self-governing arrangements rather than controlling arrangements, and the returns to shareholders could be improved by the cooperative behavior of the management. Thus, it can be concluded that the stewardship theory provides useful suggestions for establishing sustainable management, in which management plays an important role in converting conflicts among multiple goals into a constructive cooperation.

The study then focuses on the roles of the boards of directors in achieving improved sustainability performance. Japan's Corporate Governance Code fundamentally followed shareholder primacy norms and recommended prescriptions for agency theory. In addition, the shareholder primacy norm prevailed in the Companies Act. However, it became clear that the Companies Act did not exclude any CSR management, and the directors could include CSR in their management to a reasonable extent, even if shareholders' profits were sacrificed. It was also confirmed that there is a positive relationship between CSR and financial performance. Thus, we can expect the directors to manage CSR while seeking profitable solutions to the problems of the people and the planet.

Finally, the study considered different ways of thinking based on agency theory. Corporations are commitment devices rather than control devices. A corporation is not a mere private entity but a public entity. Corporate directors are not agents of shareholders but trustees who have responsibilities to act on behalf of multiple parties. Corporate directors owe their fiduciary duties to the corporation. Thus, the author considers corporations to be based on a partnership of equals. From the perspective of sustainable management, directors ought to be required to run a company while serving the interests of not only shareholders but other stakeholders as well.

References

Blair, M. M. and Stout, L. A. (1999). A Team Production Theory of Corporate Law, *Virginia Law Review*, **85**(2), 247–328.

Bowles, S. (2016). *The Moral Economy: Why Good Incentives Are No Substitute for Good Citizens*, Yale University Press, New Haven and London.

Donaldson, L. and Davis J. H. (1991). Stewardship Theory or Agency Theory: CEO Governance and Shareholder Returns, *Australian Journal of Management*, **16**(1), 49–64.

Davis, J. H., Schoorman, F. D., and Donaldson, L. (1997). Toward a Stewardship Theory of Management, *Academy of Management Review*, **22**(1), 20–47.

Egashira, K. (2021). *Laws of Stock Corporations*, Yuhikaku, Tokyo (in Japanese).

Elkington, J. (1997). *Cannibals with Forks: The Triple Bottom Line of 21st Century Business*, Capstone Publishing Ltd., Oxford.

Ito, K. (2021). *Corporate Value Management*, Nikkei Business Publications, Inc., Tokyo (in Japanese).

Iwai, K. (2009). *What Will Happen to the Company in the Future*, Heibonsha, Tokyo (in Japanese).

Japan's Corporate Governance Code (2021). Tokyo Stock Exchange, Inc., Tokyo (in Japanese).

Guidelines for Investor and Company Engagement (2021). Financial Services Agency, Tokyo (in Japanese).

Jensen, M. C. and Meckling, W. H. (1976). Theory of the Firm: Managerial Behavior, Agency Costs and Ownership Structure, *Journal of Financial Economics*, **3**, 305–360.

Mayer, C. (2018). *Prosperity: Better Business Makes the Greater Good*, Oxford University Press, Oxford.

McGuire, J. B., Sundgren, A., and Schneeweis, T. (1988). Corporate Social Responsibility and Firm Financial Performance, *Academy of Management Journal*, **31**(4), 854–872.

Miyajima, H. and Saito, T. (2020). Corporate Governance Reform under Abenomics: What Did the Two Codes Bring, *Shouji Houmu*, No. 2224, 12–23 (in Japanese).

Monden, Y. (1978). *Multi-Goal, Multi-Level Managerial Accounting*, Dobunkan, Tokyo (in Japanese).

Monden, Y. (2017). Solving the Wage Differentials Throughout the Supply Chain by Collaborative Innovations for Changing the Parts Prices and Costs, in Hamada, K. and Hiraoka, S., eds., *Japanese Management and International Studies*, Vol. 13, World Scientific Publishing Ltd., Singapore, 67–93.

Morimoto, K. (2019). Goal Congruence between Top Management and Divisional Managers, in Suzuki, K. and Gurd, B., eds., *Japanese Management and International Studies*, Vol. 15, World Scientific Publishing Ltd., Singapore, 117–131.

Stead, J. G. and Stead, W. E. (2014). *Sustainable Strategic Management*, 2nd ed., Greenleaf Publishing Ltd., Sheffield.

Tanaka, W. (2020). The Rationality and Limitations of the Shareholder Primacy, *Houritsu Jihou*, **92**(7), 79–86 (in Japanese).

Tanaka, W. (2021). *Corporate Law*, University of Tokyo Press, Tokyo (in Japanese).

Tanimoto, K. (2020). *Business and Society*, Chuokeizai, Tokyo (in Japanese).

Waddock, S. A. and Graves, S. B. (1997). The Corporate Social Performance-Financial Performance Link, *Strategic Management Journal*, **18**(4), 303–319.

Chapter 4

Multi-objective Corporate Behavior Model for Sustainable Management: Evaluation Method and the Selection and Search for a Solution

Hiroshi Ozawa

Nagoya University, Nagoya, Japan

1. Introduction

In the past 20 years, cooperative social responsibility (CSR) and sustainable development goals (SDGs) have been propagated. Companies are expected to satisfy the diverse demands of their shareholders, employees, residents, consumers, and other stakeholders. Under these circumstances, it has become challenging to explain corporate behavior only by the traditional corporate view that "the purpose of a corporation is to maximize profits" or by simplistic models of corporate behavior in economics.

In the case of a single objective, a behavioral model that seeks to "maximize" a measure of its achievement is simple. However, in the case of multiple objectives, it is almost impossible to maximize all objectives simultaneously because conflicts may occur, such as when objectives compete for scarce resources. Models of corporate behavior that assume the maximization of a single objective cannot describe the process of resolving such conflicts. Therefore, this study attempts to explain the principle of corporate behavior when a company tries to "satisfy" multiple objectives simultaneously.[1]

Maximizing and satisfying behavior naturally differ in the way performance is evaluated. Simply put, maximizing behavior evaluates the "level" of achievement, while satisfying behavior evaluates the "probability" of attainment. Moreover, the severity of the required (judgment) level in the case of assessing probability can significantly impact the estimated company's (or its employees') attitude toward risk, which can lead to corporate accidents and scandals. Therefore, this study also refers to searching for solutions to satisfy various objectives while avoiding hazards.

The content of this study consists of March and Simon's (1993) model of corporate behavior, combined with the probability valuation methods (Ozawa, 2016) and multi-objective optimization theories (Dub, 2001; Kuroiwa *et al.*, 2003; Morgan and Liker, 2006; Word and Sobek II, 2014).

2. From Single Object to Multi-objects

2.1 *The concept of profit*

The economic proposition that "corporations act to maximize profit" is widely accepted. However, this proposition does not mean that corporations have only a single objective. In fact, economics also argues that corporations pursue multiple goals. Nonetheless, it is convenient and sufficient for economics to express only the results of corporate decision-making using the concept of "profit" because the primary purpose of economics is to describe the mechanisms of the market. For this reason, decision-making and converting multiple objectives into a one-dimensional scalar are not the subject of interest in economics (Cyert and March, 1963, pp. 8–10).

---

[1]If the ratio between objectives is given and can be expressed by a linear equation, it is not included in the multi-objective in this study.

Moreover, the concept of profit is abstract and non-operational and cannot be directly measured or evaluated.[2] Therefore, when a company's decision-making process is the subject of consideration, it is necessary to identify the individual sub-objectives and describe in detail what the balance between them should be.

Considering the behavioral principle of the company's satisfaction of multiple objectives is not to deny the profit maximization but refers to unexpressed parts of the process. If a company determines the balance between the levels of achievement of multiple objectives, there must be some single objective that guarantees that the balance is desirable. We can call it "profit" or, for example, "blended value" (if profit has a strong nuance of an aim for investors or shareholders), to refer to the company's total value to all stakeholders.[3] The aim is to depict a decision-making process that does not directly pursue the maximization of a single objective. Instead, it tries to indirectly maximize a single objective while balancing multiple objectives.

3. Performance Evaluation

The performance evaluation methods to be employed differ between maximizing and satisfying actions. Additionally, in the case of satisfying action, the choice of the actor for risk varies depending on the severity of the required (judgment) level.

3.1 *Two methods of performance evaluation*

Although not widely recognized, there are two performance evaluation methods (Ozawa, 2016). These two methods do not have common names.

---

[2] Profit in economics and profit in accounting are different concepts. Profit in economics cannot be directly measured and evaluated, while in accounting, it can be measured and evaluated as the difference between revenues and expenses. They also differ in the period assumed. Profit in accounting is the difference between revenues and expenses, usually for one year, whereas in economics, it is the sum of incentives earned over an unlimited future period.

[3] Blended value is a concept presented in Emerson (2003, p. 45) that integrates the economic, social, and environmental values created by a company.

Therefore, they will be referred to as *the level evaluation* and *the probability evaluation* methods in this study.[4]

The level evaluation method in this study is a method in which goals relate to levels, and the achievement levels also evaluate performance. For example, when the target level is 60 points, and the achievement level is 80 points, the evaluation is "20 points above the target." In the probability evaluation method, the judgment level is first set. Goals are then given regarding probability or how often the achievement level exceeds the judgment level and are also evaluated according to the probability or frequency. For example, in the above example, the evaluation "exceeded the judgment level." In other cases, the probability of achievement or the number of triumphs is used as the evaluation value, such as "succeeded seven times out of 10 times." In this case, whether or not the judgment level was exceeded is determined by a binary value, and it does not matter by how much the achievement exceeded the judgment level.

Simply, maximizing behavior means maximizing levels. In this case, the level evaluation method is used. In the case of satisfying behavior, the probability evaluation method is used because the probability or the number of times the judgment level is satisfied is evaluated, not the height of the achievement level.

The expression "target level" is used only in the level evaluation method. In the probability evaluation method, the target is given in terms of the probability or number of times of achievement rather than the level. Therefore, the expression "judgment level," "required level," "acceptable level," or "standard" is used instead of "target level."

3.2 *Confusion between target level and judgment level*

It is a well-known hypothesis that "goals should be at a difficult but attainable level" (Ach, 1910; Locke *et al.*, 1910; McClelland, 1987; March and Simon, 1993; Larnick *et al.*, 1999). The intent is to encourage above-normal effort by setting a goal at a level that cannot be achieved through

---

[4]Another possible method is to combine the two methods and evaluate the product of the level of achievement and the probability of achievement.

normal behavior.[5] While this phrase is accurate in the context of the level evaluation method, it cannot simply be applied to the context of the probability evaluation method.

Figure 1 shows two points, E and s, on the horizontal axis representing the level of performance. Point E is the average past performance and expected future level (average expected level). Point s is a more challenging level. In the context of the level evaluation method, this point is said to be a "difficult but attainable level." Therefore, this relationship $(s > E)$ would be felt reasonable and would not be questioned in many cases.

The magnitude of outcomes, incidentally, varies because it is affected by various factors. Therefore, Figure 2(a) superimposes a normal distribution on this axis, assuming that this variation follows a normal distribution. By doing so, our thinking switches from the level evaluation method to the probability evaluation method, giving a different impression from that in Figure 1.

In the probability evaluation method, when $s > E$, the probability that the achievement level exceeds the judgment level (s) (the shaded area in the figure) is always less than 50%. In other words, the probability of

Figure 1.   Expected and Target Levels

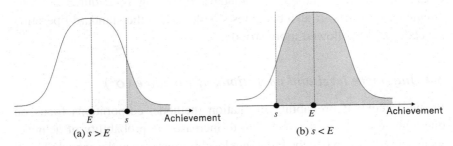

(a) $s > E$ (b) $s < E$

Figure 2.   Probability Distribution and Probability of Achievement

---

[5] In March and Simon (1993, p. 205), it is introduced as "the concept of optimal stress."

non-achievement is greater than the probability of achievement. Conversely, when $s < E$, the probability that the achievement level exceeds the judgment level (s) is always greater than 50% (Figure 2(b)). In other words, the probability of achievement is greater than the probability of non-achievement. Figure 2 clearly shows the results when a "difficult goal ($s > E$)" is given.

3.3 *Two variables affecting probability of achievement*

The probability evaluation method aims to increase the area to the right of s in Figure 2. Therefore, when the probability evaluation method is employed, the evaluator (company or employee) increases the probability of achievement. In other words, Figure 2 shows the distribution before the evaluator takes such action (prior distribution) and the distribution after the action (posterior distribution) should be different.

   If we maintain the assumption that the variability of outcomes follows a normal distribution, its shape is specified by two variables: the mean or expected level (E) and the variance (σ^2). The expected level (E) is determined by structural determinants of corporate behavior, such as standard operating procedures. These can be changed in the long run but should be considered as given in the short run.

   In contrast, the variance (σ^2) is the deviation from the expected level (E). This is caused by actions that are not determined by standard operating procedures. In other words, there is room for discretion. Therefore, the clearer and more detailed the standard operating procedures are, the smaller it becomes. It also becomes smaller when the standard operating procedures are followed more strictly.

3.4 *Judgment level and operations of variance (σ^2)*

In the context of probability evaluation methods, corporations focus on operating variance in the short run to increase the probability of achievement. In this case, when the judgment level is greater than the expected level ($s > E$) or smaller ($s < E$), the corporation's choice for risk is different.

   When the judgment level is greater than the expected level ($s > E$), the probability of achievement is increased by increasing the variance

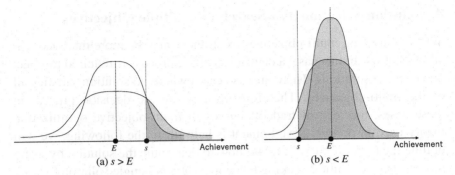

(a) *s* > *E*   (b) *s* < *E*

Figure 3.   Judgment Level and Operations of Variance

(Figure 3(a)). For example, the strictness of compliance with standard operating procedures may be loosened, such as by using different procedures for operations than in the past. This method increases the probability of achievement, but at the same time, it also increases the probability of achieving a lower level of results than before; in other words, setting $s > E$ forces the actor to choose innovative and risky actions.[6]

Conversely, when the judgment level is lower than the expected level ($s < E$), decreasing the variance increases the probability of achievement. For example, one can increase the rigor of compliance with standard operating procedures by being careful or by accurately repeating the conventional way of doing things; in other words, making $s < E$ forces the actor to choose controlled and low-risk actions. In this case, a high level of performance is not achieved, but it does not mean that the actor did not try. Instead of increasing the performance level, the action is directed toward improving the probability of achievement.

Thus, in the context of the probability evaluation method, $s > E$ induces the actor to choose innovative and risky behavior. In contrast, $s < E$ causes the actor to select controlled and low-risk behavior, which is the exact opposite.

---

[6] March and Simon (1993) argue that "innovation will be most rapid and vigorous when the 'stress' on the organization is neither too high nor too low. By stress is meant the discrepancy between the level of aspiration and the level of achievement (p. 205)," and suggest that a moderately high judgment level may induce a different and innovative behavior.

4. Solution Selection and Search in Multiple Objectives

When competing multi-objectives exist, there may be more than one fea-sible solution. In this case, a decision-making process is required to select one of these solutions. There are also cases where no solution satisfies all of the multi-objectives. Therefore, to describe the decision process in these cases, the idea of tradeoff curves in multi-objective optimization theory used in product development is helpful. In the following, we will outline the tradeoff curve, explain how to determine the solution by using it, and discuss solution-seeking behavior when no single solution exists.

4.1 *Tradeoff curves*

In the product development process, tradeoff curves are used to determine the level of each factor while balancing multiple competing factors that affect product value, such as weight, cost, robustness, quietness, and other functions. A tradeoff curve is a formula or graph that expresses the rela-tionship between design factors and product value. The tradeoff curve concept was developed for product development. It can also be applied to other corporate decision-making where subordinate objectives are divided from a singular objective in a competitive relationship.

Figure 4 is an example of a tradeoff curve. It represents the relationship between the magnitude of the springback (a phenomenon of a metal sheet attempting to recover when it comes off the die) and the two factors that affect

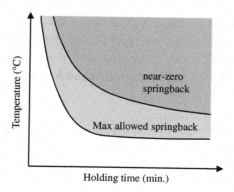

Figure 4.   Tradeoff Curve

Source: Partially modified from Ward and Sobek II (2014, p. 160).

it when a metal sheet is pressed and formed. The vertical axis indicates the heating temperature of the metal sheet, and the horizontal axis indicates the holding time. Of the two curves in the figure, the upper right represents the combination of heating temperature and holding time at which springback is almost zero. Increasing the holding time or heating temperature beyond this curve does not increase the effect. The lower left curve shows the maximum amount of springback that can be tolerated or the lower permissible limit. A solution is selected from the possible combinations of holding time and heating temperature shown in this figure.

The setting of the lower permissible limit is critical in tradeoff curves. When multiple factors are considered simultaneously, it is necessary to initially set the requirement level at the lower permissible limit and prepare as many solution options as possible. The requirement level is then gradually raised while considering the relationship with each factor, and one solution is selected while narrowing down the options.

Suppose we replace the springback size (or the value of the product), which is the higher objective in this process, with the "profit (or the blended value)." In that case, we can describe the behavior of a company pursuing the most desirable state while pursuing multiple objectives, such as financial outcome, protection of the natural environment, improvement of employment conditions, and so on. In the case of product development, however, most of the variables used to create the tradeoff curve and the factors that influence them are operational concepts. Additionally, the company can use physical and engineering laws and test data. In contrast, measuring stakeholder satisfaction and identifying its influencing factors are difficult. Therefore, challenges remain in applying this method to corporate behavior and making it practical.

4.2 *Solution selection*

Figure 5 shows the two competing objectives of a company and the set of solutions that could simultaneously achieve them. The horizontal and vertical axes show the competing objectives A and B (for example, economic performance and social performance) and the levels (E_A, E_B) expected to be achieved on average if each objective were pursued alone (corresponding to point E in Figure 3). Curve L represents the combination of objectives A and B with equal profit (or the blended value). In the case of this figure, the higher the right, the greater the profit ($L_1 < L_2$).

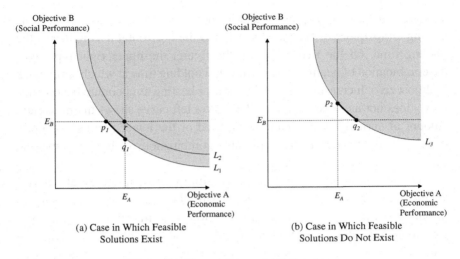

Figure 5.   Range of Acceptable Solutions

For example, curve L_1 in Figure 5(a) is the lower permissible limit of profit, i.e., the minimum required for a combination of objectives A and B. Therefore, to avoid stakeholder dissatisfaction, the combination of objectives A and B must be determined within the shaded range to the upper right. On curve L_1, the thick line between p_1 and q_1 is the set of possible solutions. If there is such a choice of solutions, the profit level can be raised from L_1 to L_2, for example. This way, the possible levels of objectives A and B, i.e., the solutions, are narrowed down.

Contrary to this, curve L_3 in Figure 5(b) shows a situation where the lower permissible profit limit is more severe than L_1 and L_2. In this case, no profit solution is below the average expected level (E_A, E_B) of objectives A and B. Therefore, perhaps the point p_2, where objective A can be achieved but not objective B, or the point q_2, where objective B can be achieved but not objective A, or a midpoint between p_2 and q_2, which is both pain points, is selected. In this case, the solution cannot be found via analytical methods, and the political process chooses the answer, such as (a) persuasion, (b) negotiation, and (c) political strategy[7] (March and Simon, 1993, pp. 149–151).

---

[7] The decision mechanism through the political process is detailed in Pfeffer (1992).

4.3 *Searching for new solutions*

In the context of the probability evaluation method, any point between p_2 and q_2 will result in a more demanding level of either or both objectives A and B than the average expectation level (E_A, E_B). This causes corporations to choose innovative and risky actions. This could lead to corporate accidents and corporate scandals.

There are two ways for corporations to find feasible solutions while avoiding risky behavior. One is for corporations to review their standard operating procedures to improve E_A and E_B. However, as already mentioned, this would take a long time. The other way is to vary the tradeoff curve by taking into account, in addition to objectives A and B, another factor closely related to them (factor X). This may allow lowering the lower permissible profit limit, L_3, to the level of L'_3 or L''_3 (Figure 6(a)) or changing the judgment level E_A and E_B (Figure 6(b)).

In Figure 5, only the relationship between objectives A and B is shown, but Figure 6(a) shows how the curve L_3 moves to the lower left by changing the level of factor X, and Figure 6(b) shows how E_A and E_B are changed. Thus, we may be able to generate solutions to existing objectives

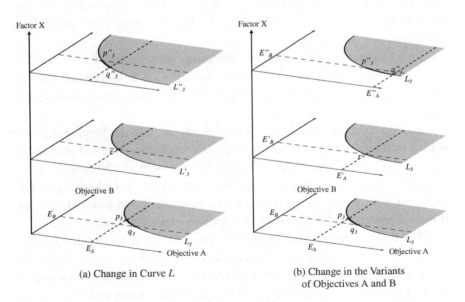

(a) Change in Curve *L*

(b) Change in the Variants of Objectives A and B

Figure 6. Shift of Requirement Level due to Pluralization

A and B by considering other factors and changing the level of these factors, which we have not considered so far.

However, factor X is often outside the control of the corporation, for example, the characteristics of raw materials and components that the company depends on, the level of environmental regulations the government or industry sets, or the level of customer requirements. In most cases, corporations cannot achieve all their objectives in a self-contained manner, so they must now act as a stakeholder, reaching out to other organizations to influence strategic factors outside their control. Traditionally, the approach by an organization to other organizations has been discussed as an environmental management strategy and explained as an action of uncertainty reduction (Kobashi, 1998, 1999a, 1999b, 2001). The model in this study indicates the possibility that the approach to other organizations may occur while also searching for an acceptable solution.

5. Conclusion

In this study, we have presented a model of corporate behavior when simultaneously pursuing multiple objectives when responding to the diverse demands of various stakeholders. The following three points are discussed.

First, when pursuing multiple objectives simultaneously, the model should be based not on maximizing the level of achievement but on increasing the probability of satisfying a given level (satisfying behavior).

Second, performance evaluation methods include the level and probability evaluation methods. The probability evaluation method should be used in the case of satisfying behavior. In this method, the firm chooses innovative and risky actions if the judgment level exceeds the average expected level. Conversely, it decides on controlled and low-risk actions if the judgment level is less than the average expected level.

The third point of discussion is the process of narrowing down solutions in order to select one. When multiple solutions exist, the profit curve should be raised to narrow down the solution. When no solution exists, there are two methods: one is to solve the problem self-sufficiently through innovative and risky behavior and the other is to change the tradeoff curve or factor variables by working with external organizations while keeping control behavior. Among these methods, the solution using innovative behavior can result in corporate accidents and corporate scandals.

The corporate behavior model in this study enables us to explain more complex corporate behavior than ever. And incidentally, it also suggests that searching for satisfactory solutions may motivate environmental management strategy.

References

Ach, N. (1910). *Über die Willensakt und das Temperament*, Quelle and Meyer, Leipzig.

Cyert, R. M. and March, J. G. (1963). *A Behavioral Theory of the Firm*, Prentice-Hall, New Jersey.

Dub, K. (2001). *Multi-objective Optimization Using Evolutionary Algorithms*, John Wiley & Sons, New Jersey.

Emerson, J. (2003). The Blended Value Proposition: Integrating Social and Financial Returns, *California Management Review*, **45**(4), 35–51.

Kobashi, T. (1998). Mechanisms of Environmental Management Strategy: From the Standpoint of Uncertainty and Interdependence, *The Economic Science*, **46**(1), 57–70 (in Japanese).

Kobashi, T. (1999a). The Organization's Environment and Environmental Management Strategy: An Analysis of the Organization's Strategy concerning Inter-organizational Relations, D. dissertation, Graduate School of Economics, Nagoya University (in Japanese).

Kobashi, T. (1999b). Environmental Management Strategy: The Analysis of Loosening Strategy, *The Economic Science*, **47**(3), 91–104 (in Japanese).

Kobashi, T. (2001). The Process of Implementation of Environmental Management Strategy: From the Standpoint of Sensemaking of Environment, *The Economic Science*, **48**(4), 117–130 (in Japanese).

Kuroiwa, T., Furukawa, R. and Oitomi, K. (2003). Applicability of Multi-objective Optimization to Functional Design Process, *Proceedings of the 13th Annual Conference of the Japan Society of Mechanical Engineers*, Design Engineering and Systems Division, pp. 106–107 (in Japanese).

Larnick, R., Wu, G. and Heath, C. (1999). Rising the Bar on Goals, Graduate School of Business Publication, University of Chicago, Spring.

Locke, E. A., Shaw, K. N., Saari, L. M. and Latham, G. P. (1980). Goal Setting and Task Performance: 1969–1980 (Tech. Rep. for the Organizational Effectiveness Research Program), Office of Naval Research, Washington, D. C.

March, J. G. and Simon, H. A. (1993). *Organizations*, 2nd ed., Blackwell Publishers, Cambridge, MA.

McClelland, D. C. (1987). *Human Motivation*, Cambridge University Press, Cambridge, UK.

Morgan, J. M. and Liker, J. K. (2006). *The Toyota Product Development System: Integrating People, Process, and Technology*, Productivity Press, New York.

Ozawa, H. (2016). Control, Improvement, Innovation and Performance Evaluation Methods, *Sangyo-keiri*, **76**(4), 80–92 (in Japanese).

Pfeffer, J. (1992). *Managing with Power*, Harvard Business School Press, Boston.

Ward, A. C. and Sobek II, D. K. (2014). *Lean Product and Process Development*, 2nd ed., Lean Enterprise Institute, Cambridge, MA.

Part 2

Practical Examples of Sustainability Management in Japan

Chapter 5

The Study of Japanese Companies' Per Hour Labor Productivity

Shufuku Hiraoka

Soka University, Tokyo, Japan

1. Introduction

Generally, studies clarifying the relationship between work duration and productivity in Japan thus far have had the following characteristics:

(1) macro-level analytical comparison of countries' indexes,
(2) references to case studies of Japanese companies under micro-level analysis, e.g., Kyocera Corp.

Some previous studies have also analyzed the relationship between work duration and productivity in Japan. However, few studies have investigated the relationship between time labor productivity and the corporate profitability index.

Sustainability investing, also known as environmental, social, and governance (ESG) investing, has recently garnered attention and is related to the sustainable development goals (SDGs). The study of time labor productivity is closely connected with Goal 8. Therefore, we should clarify whether time labor productivity impacts the stock price-related index.

71

This research used a proxy variable given the difficulty of strictly measuring the productivity indexes because of disclosure constraints. In this chapter, the author analyzes the impact of the proxy variable for time labor productivity on profitability and the stock price-related index. Finally, results-based implications for Japanese companies regarding solving some of the problems they face are shared.

2. Research Background

The novel coronavirus (COVID-19) has largely impacted — and continues to affect — many Japanese companies. However, it is very difficult to measure its influence on productivity under the circumstances. Productivity can be measured according to some factors, such as sales, operating profit, labor costs, interest, dividends, and taxes. Calculating operating profit before taxes entails consideration of interest, dividends, and taxes. Labor costs are subtracted from the gross margin when calculating operating profit. Therefore, we used the sum of labor costs and operating profit as a proxy variable of value-added because due to disclosure constraints, we could not use the value-added less material costs from sales. Furthermore, because of COVID-19's enormous influence, we analyzed pre-COVID-19 data.

Presently, many Japanese companies and the government are focusing on reducing working hours under the work reform system and amidst digitization. Accordingly, we used time labor productivity as a proxy variable. Even if per person productivity increases with a given number of employees, time labor productivity might not increase in the presence of long working hours. Many employees will be exhausted in such an environment, which will lower productivity. Improving time labor productivity is one of the best ways to achieve sustainable employees.

3. Survey of Previous Research

Cascio (2006) compared the per hour salary difference between Walmart and Costco and found that the higher the per hour salary, the higher the operating profit. Per hour salary is the first factor comprising per hour time labor productivity, and operating profit is the second factor.

According to Strain (2019), employee salary growth rate is related to that of productivity. Lazear (2000) showed that the shift from piecework to a per hour salary improved productivity at Safelite Glass Corp. We can assert that an employee can earn a higher per hour salary if they can produce a larger volume within the same number of hours. Sato (2008) pointed out that working hours will lengthen when employees want to work until they achieve the desired results.

Ono (2018) enumerated the disadvantages of long working hours and workdays as follows:

(1) Long workdays produce waste and inefficiency with respect to human capital.
(2) Long workdays make it difficult for employees to balance work and life.
(3) Long workdays slow the progress of diversity.
(4) Long workdays could restrain innovation.
(5) Long working hours negatively affect well-being.

Additionally, he indicated the necessity of a specific measurement index related to the shift from input to output toward shortening working hours and workdays.

According to research conducted by the Cabinet Office (2017), the shorter an employee's working hours, the higher the per person productivity. In 2015, total working hours in Japan were about 1.25 times those of Germany, and Germany's per person productivity exceeded Japan's by nearly 50%. When applying this principle to the correlation between per person hours of labor and labor productivity, it is estimated that a 10% reduction in an employee's working hours produces a 25% improvement in labor productivity. Many companies expect hybridized telework to increase productivity. Japan reported a 10% reduction in working hours and a 20% improvement in labor productivity during the 20 years spanning 1995–2015. However, Germany and France reported that labor productivity increased by 30% during the same period. Although the reduction in hours of labor in Sweden and the United States was smaller than that in Japan, those countries' labor productivity grew by 40%.

According to Yamamoto and Kuroda (2014), Japan's per hour labor productivity ranked 19th among Organization for Economic Cooperation and Development (OECD) member countries. In 2016, Maeda (2018) showed that Japan's per hour labor productivity ranked 20th among OECD member countries and that Japan was the least productive of the G7 nations, among which the shorter the working hours, the higher the per hour time labor productivity.

Suda *et al.*'s (2011) empirical study confirmed strong relationships between average annual salary and market capitalization and sales per employee, respectively. However, their research did not include a working hours index.

In the area of management accounting, some studies have investigated the relationship between working hours and productivity. Hamada (1989) was the first to examine per hour value-added considering labor costs in the case of Kyocera. Mizuno (2013) posited labor costs as a result distributed from value-added. Mizushima (2015) also emphasized the importance of per hour value-added through the case of Kyocera.

Unfortunately, none of the abovementioned studies explained the level of per hour time labor productivity as a benchmark index for specific industries or across all industries. In the case of Japan, the differences between industries and the gap between companies have not yet been explained. How strong are the relationships between per hour time labor productivity and profitability and stock indexes, respectively? The uniqueness of this research lies in its attempt to answer that question.

4. Empirical Research

4.1 *Data sources and target period*

This research referenced the following data sources:

(1) CSR Data Book, 2018–2021,
(2) Stock Price Data Book, 2018–2021,
(3) Corporate Financial Karte, 2018–2021.

The above are special editions of *Weekly Toyo Keizai*. We obtained the following indexes from those data sources:

(1) average annual salary per person,
(2) average annual total working hours per person,
(3) per person operating profit,
(4) sales per person,
(5) net assets per share,
(6) number of employees at the end of the period,
(7) return on equity,
(8) return on assets,
(9) return on sales,
(10) closing stock price at the end of the period.

Table 1 shows the number of companies that we obtained each year. All companies are listed on the stock exchange in Japan.

4.2 *Calculating per hour labor productivity*

Per hour labor productivity comprises the following two factors:

(1) average salary per working hour (ASPH),
(2) operating profit per working hour (OPH).

The sum of (1) and (2) is the proxy variable for per hour labor productivity.

Table 1. Number of Companies with All the Data

Year	Number of Companies
2016	508
2017	609
2018	671
2019	730
Total	2,518

The amount distributed to suppliers represents sales of supplies, which produce salaries and the operating profit on supplies. Sales per working hour (SPH) roughly constitute a productivity index for measuring customer value. However, the correlation coefficient of ASPH and SPH for the period 2016–2019 was 0.268, while that of OPH and SPH was 0.303, neither of which is significant. Therefore, we excluded SPH from our analysis. Although a significant correlation may be found in some industries, this research did not consider that possibility. We measured per hour labor productivity as follows based on the available data:

Per hour labor productivity
  = Average annual salary per person
    ÷ Average annual total working hours per person
    + Per person operating profit
    ÷Average annual total working hours per person

In this study, the productivity distribution factors were salary, interest, dividends, taxes, and retained earnings, where salary is a distribution source for employees and operating profit is a source for distributing other factors.

4.3 *Average per hour labor productivity and country ranking*

Table 2 shows the average per hour labor productivity and the ranking by industry for the period 2016–2019. The difference between the maximum and the minimum tends to widen year by year. Among 29 industries, only nine (i.e., mining, real estate, oil and coal, pharmaceuticals, banking, other finance, construction, chemistry, and telecommunications), representing 31% of all industries, had an above-average value.

4.4 *Relationship between per hour labor productivity and profitability*

Are per hour labor productivity and profitability correlated? Table 3 shows the correlation coefficients between per labor productivity and the profitability indexes (ROE, ROA, and ROS).

Table 2. Average Per Hour Labor Productivity and Ranking

Type of Industry	Labor Productivity Per Hour (Yen)	Rank	Type of Industry	Labor Productivity Per Hour (Yen)	Rank
Oil & coal	11,832	3	Transportation & warehouse	5,286	14
Pharmaceuticals	9,872	4	Machine	5,051	17
Mining	39,367	1	Telecommunications	5,877	9
Real estate	19,716	2	Land transportation	5,517	13
Wholesale	5,779	10	Non-ferrous metal	4,797	20
Fisheries	5,005	18	Other products	4,124	24
Construction	6,555	7	Fiber products	4,357	22
Electrical equipment	4,776	21	Pulp & paper	4,122	25
Other finance	9,716	6	Transportation equipment	4,128	23
Electricity & gas	5,650	11	Steel	4,107	26
Bank	9,797	5	Rubber products	3,907	28
Precision equipment	4,928	19	Metal product	3,646	29
Chemistry	6,253	8	Service	5,166	16
Foods	5,587	12	Retailing	4,075	27
Glass, earth & stone	5,232	15	Average	5,869	

Table 3. Correlation Coefficients Between Per Hour Labor Productivity and Profitability

Type of Industry	Labor Productivity Per hour (Yen)	Rank	The Correlation Coefficient						Number of Samples
			ROE	Rank	ROS	Rank	ROA	Rank	
Oil & coal	11,832	3	0.559	6	0.878	6	0.877	1	12
Real estate	19,716	2	0.369	17	0.848	7	0.340	19	38
Pharmaceuticals	9,872	4	0.791	2	0.909	4	0.842	3	75

(Continued)

Table 3. *(Continued)*

Type of Industry	Labor Productivity Per hour (Yen)	Rank	The Correlation Coefficient						Number of Samples
			ROE	Rank	ROS	Rank	ROA	Rank	
Mining	39,367	1	0.269	22	0.995	1	0.258	22	8
Wholesale	5,779	11	0.450	11	0.180	28	0.360	18	178
Construction	6,555	7	0.073	27	0.468	24	0.249	24	150
Electrical equipment	4,776	21	0.314	18	0.707	18	0.612	8	277
Fisheries	5,005	18	−0.152	29	0.753	14	0.542	12	7
Bank	9,797	5	0.095	26	0.285	27	0.027	28	49
Chemistry	6,253	8	0.503	9	0.801	11	0.684	6	250
Other finance	9,716	6	−0.116	28	−0.089	29	0.035	27	45
Electricity & gas	5,950	9	0.396	15	0.648	20	0.170	25	44
Foods	5,587	12	0.711	3	0.812	9	0.698	5	141
Glass, earth & stone	5,232	15	0.285	19	0.419	25	0.252	23	39
Transportation & warehouse	5,286	14	0.242	24	0.879	5	0.140	26	93
Precision equipment	4,928	19	0.538	7	0.547	23	0.520	13	43
Machine	5,051	17	0.285	19	0.797	12	0.484	15	148
Telecommunications	5,877	10	0.259	23	0.644	21	0.265	21	178
Land transportation	5,517	13	0.438	14	0.949	2	0.316	20	60
Non-ferrous metal	4,797	20	0.511	8	0.787	13	0.548	10	47
Fiber products	4,357	22	0.884	1	0.846	8	0.847	2	39
Other products	4,124	24	0.632	5	0.718	16	0.666	7	75
Steel	4,107	26	0.696	4	0.922	3	0.748	4	33
Transportation equipment	4,128	23	0.283	21	0.590	22	0.451	16	149
Rubber products	3,907	28	0.442	12	0.718	16	0.559	9	36
Pulp & paper	4,122	25	0.177	25	0.402	26	−0.129	29	25
Metal product	3,646	29	0.501	10	0.802	10	0.545	11	42
Service	5,166	16	0.390	16	0.750	15	0.429	17	153
Retailing	4,075	27	0.440	13	0.701	19	0.498	14	144
All industries	5,869		0.073		0.606		0.217		2,518

The correlation coefficient between per hour labor productivity and ROS was the highest (0.606), based on data for all industries. Among 29 industries, 21 had a correlation coefficient above 0.606.

Regarding specific industries, fiber products had the highest correlation coefficient between per hour labor productivity and ROE (0.884).

In pharmaceuticals, the correlation coefficients between per hour labor productivity and ROE, ROS, and ROA were 0.791, 0.909, and 0.842, respectively (with 75 samples). For the food industry, the correlation coefficient between per hour labor productivity and ROE was 0.711 (with 141 samples). In the steel industry, the correlation coefficients between per hour labor productivity and ROA and ROE were 0.748 and 0.696, respectively. For other products, the correlation coefficient between per hour labor productivity and ROA was 0.847. In four industries, namely oil and coal, fiber products, pharmaceuticals, and steel, the correlation coefficients between per hour labor productivity and ROA were just over 0.7. In conclusion, correlations were found between per hour labor productivity and profitability indexes in Japan, and there exists disparity between industries.

4.5 Relationship between per hour labor productivity and some indexes related to stock price

Finally, the author analyzes the relationship between per hour labor productivity and some indexes related to fiscal year-end stock price during the period 2017–2019.

The land transportation industry had the highest correlation coefficient between per hour labor productivity and stock price (0.844). That of the transportation and warehousing industry was also very high (0.822). In the fiber products industry, the correlation coefficient between per hour labor productivity and the Price Book-Value Ratio (PBR) value ratio was 0.735. The high correlation coefficients between per labor productivity and stock price at the 2017 fiscal year end are shown in Table 4.

No positive correlation coefficients between per hour labor productivity and indexes related to stock price were found using the data covering all industries. However, we found positive correlations in some industries.

Table 4. Relationship With Stock Price as of March 31, 2018

Industry	Correlation Coefficient
Food	0.962
Land transportation	0.851
Retail	0.839
Wholesale	0.811

5. Summary and Remaining Issues

In this study, the author calculated per hour labor productivity with a proxy variable. The relationships between per hour labor productivity and profitability and indexes related to stock price were analyzed, respectively. Given the restrictions on the available data, the sample size was 2,518 for the period 2016–2019. The sum of average salary and operating profit per working hour was available as a proxy variable for per hour labor productivity. The difference between the maximum and the minimum tended to increase year by year in all industries, despite the disparity between industries. That trend may be intensifying amidst the COVID-19 crisis.

The immediate goal of this study was to examine the correlation between per hour labor productivity and profitability and indexes related to stock price, respectively. According to the data for all industries, ROS was strongly correlated with per hour labor productivity. In addition to ROS, ROE and ROA had high correlation coefficients with per hour labor productivity in fiber products, pharmaceuticals, food, steel, and other products. The correlation between per hour labor productivity and stock price was also strong in transportation and warehousing, including land transportation. A similarly high correlation was found in fiber products. Other products, electrical equipment, transportation equipment, and fiber products had correlation coefficients between per hour labor productivity and stock price in the range of 0.5–0.6. Regarding other products, per hour labor productivity was positively correlated with PBR. Based on the data for the 2017 fiscal year, the food, land transportation, retail, and wholesale industries had correlation coefficients over 0.8. According to the above, we can confirm positive relationships between per hour labor productivity and profitability and indexes related to stock price, respectively.

Next, the author points out some problems facing Japanese companies. The per hour labor productivity disparity among not only industries but also companies predates COVID-19. Moreover, that tendency has increased year by year, depending on the type of industry. Some industries have 10–20 times the disparity. The service industry was probably the hardest hit by COVID-19. Could we, as expected, state that Japanese employees at some service companies provide low-quality labor, even given Japan's originally low per hour labor productivity?

Finally, the remaining issues are as follows:

- The author could only obtain data for 4 years. One reason is that annual total working hours by company have only been surveyed since the 2016 fiscal year. Hence, the sample size may be insufficient. There also exist differences between industries. Moreover, many companies do not publish total annual working hours, and the distribution depends on it.
- The author could not analyze the impact of company size differences. A company size index needs to be devised to facilitate future consideration of this factor.
- Regarding the differences in labor quality, is this aspect properly evaluated? Could we state that the labor quality is low in industries and companies that currently pay a low per hour salary? Is it just that the evaluation rate is low? We should first discuss an appropriate per hour salary.
- How should data representing the COVID-19 pandemic and post-COVID-19 society be analyzed? Is the research method used in this study actually suitable, as expected?
- What is the balance between annual salary and operating profit? The correlation coefficient between annual salary ranking and that of operating profit was high (0.764) for the fiscal years 2016–2019.
- Do companies and industries in other countries face the same problems as Japanese companies, or are some problems unique to Japan?

This study could show the benchmark levels for industries and companies. Work style reform, DX, and economy recovery post-COVID-19 will affect per hour labor productivity and should receive due attention. This paper is a partial revision of Hiraoka (2022).

References

Cabinet Office (2017). The Impact of Working Style Reform on Production Activities, *Annual Economic Financial Report 2017*, pp. 107–125 (in Japanese).

Cascio, W. F. (2006). The High Cost of Low Wages, *Harvard Business Review*, December, p. 23.

Hamada, K. (1989). The Profit Management System by Amoeba Method: The Case Study of Kyocera, *Accounting*, **41**(2), 46–52 (in Japanese).

Hiraoka, S. (2022). The Study of Labor Productivity Per Person Hour: Industry Analysis for Japanese Companies Before COVID-19, *The Review of Business Administration of Soka University*, **46**(1), 27–41 (in Japanese).

Lazear, E. P. (2000). Performance, Pay and Productivity, *The American Economic Review*, **90**(5), 1346–1361.

Maeda, Y. (2018). The Current Status and Issues of Labor Productivity in Japan: Focusing Capital Investment After the Burst of the Bubble and Long Working Hours in Japan, *Legislation and Investigation*, **41**, 41–51 (in Japanese).

Mizuno, I. (2013). Management Accounting Aiming for Humanism, *Aoyama Accounting Review*, **13**, 32–39 (in Japanese).

Mizushima, T. (2015). *Time Management Accounting Theory: An Attempt at Systematic Organization*, Dobunkan. (in Japanese), Tokyo.

Ono, H. (2018). Why Do Japanese Work Long Hours? *Japan Labor Issues*, **2**(5), February–March, 34–49.

Strain, M. R. (2019). The Link Between Ages and Productivity Is Strong, *American Enterprise Institute and Institute for the Study of Labor*, pp. 169–179.

Suda, I., Hah, Y., Okuma, M., and Oshika, T. (2013). Financial Reporting Analysis from the Perspective of Empirical Research, *Transformation of Financial Reporting*, Chuo Keizai-sha, p. 74. (in Japanese).

Yamamoto, K. and Kuroda, S. (2014). *Economic Analysis of Working Time: Looking Out on How to Work in a Super Aging Society*, Nihon Keizai Shinbun Publishing. (in Japanese), Tokyo.

Chapter 6

Japanese Cost Management Based on Respect for the Humanity of Employees: The Case of Toyota

Noriyuki Imai

International Professional University of Technology in Nagoya
Aichi, Japan

1. Introduction

Traditional management accounting emphasizes cost savings in which company-wide profit planning and budgetary management control the absolute value of costs on the shop floor. In other words, cost reduction in traditional management accounting theory is the management of financial figures.

At the same time, Toyota's cost reduction in the mass production process mainly depends on the Toyota Production System (TPS). At the manufacturing site operated by TPS, employees voluntarily and actively carry out kaizen ("improvement") activities. Toyota adopts its own cost reduction, which is aimed at consolidating the cost-reduction effect (delta value) generated from employees' kaizen activities into the profit management system after the fact. In other words, cost reduction in Toyota's mass production process is primarily the management of activities.

TPS is a system that maximizes the potential of employees through the voluntary execution of kaizen activities based on Toyota's value of respecting the humanity of employees. This chapter considers the characteristics of Toyota-like cost management, which respects the humanity of employees and strives to reduce costs by managing activities.

2. Cost Reduction in Traditional Management Accounting Theory

In management accounting, the concept of profit planning and budget management sprouted in the first half of the 20th century.

Knoeppel (1930) pointed out that companies that earned profit during the Great Depression have the following two characteristics: (1) They investigated and predicted the future business environment. (2) They planned projects and set a budget. In addition, Knoeppel (1931) argued for the importance of profit planning and budget management in that a predetermined amount of profit was designated in advance and measures were planned to secure this level of profit.

In the United States after World War II, a new organizational form emerged and spread to replace the functional organization: business division organization. Simon (1960) pointed out the following three points regarding divisional organization: (1) US has achieved long-term growth through diversification. (2) Diversified companies organize business divisions by product group, consolidate related activities and operations into business divisions, and delegate authority to business divisions. (3) The business division system organization is a decentralized organizational structure that enables effective business management. According to Dean (1951), who conducted research on how to measure profits in a business unit, the introduction of the business division organization has made the method of measuring profits of business divisions an important management issue. On that basis, Dean (1951) presented the following two concepts related to "profit for control:" (1) It is appropriate to measure the profit of the business division not by net profit but by manageable profit. (2) It is appropriate to measure the profit of a business division not by the return on invested capital but by the amount of profit because the current business division manager cannot take responsibility for the investment made by the previous business division manager. Dean (1951) pioneered the concept of profit management to control the absolute value of profits.

Horngren *et al.* (1999) pointed out the following three aspects of profit planning and budget management: (1) The business plan is summarized for each organizational unit, such as sales, production, and distribution. (2) Targets related to sales, cost-driver activities, purchasing, production, net profit, etc. are quantified. (3) A forecast income statement is created, the profit plan is displayed in monetary terms, and the budget is managed.

Simons (1999), referring to profit planning and budget management, highlighted the following points: (1) The purpose of the company is to generate profits. (2) The company must predict future profits, plan profits, and manage the budget. (3) The profit target is the financial effort target presented by the management to the business division.

Okamoto *et al.* (2003) pointed out the following with regard to profit planning and budget management: (1) Many companies aim for continuous growth and value creation. (2) A company plans profits and manages its budget based on its medium- to long-term management plan. (3) The company draws the attention of employees to the profit plan, raises the motivation of employees, and orders and guides the employees to execute the profit plan and budget management. (4) The company compares the budget with the actual results, analyzes the differences, evaluates the performance of the implementer, and takes corrective measures if necessary.

Nishimura and Oshita (2007) highlighted the following points regarding profit planning and budget management: (1) Many companies achieve their management objectives through long-term stable growth. (2) The company manages profits and budgets. (3) Budget management is a management activity to achieve the profit target determined in the profit plan. (4) The budget includes those for annual sales volume, production volume, sales, purchase amount, manufacturing cost, selling expenses, and financial matters. (5) At the end of the fiscal year, the budget and actual results are compared, the performances of departments and individuals are evaluated, the cause of the difference between the budget and actual results is investigated, and the responsibility is clarified.

This overview of the concepts of profit planning and budget management in traditional management accounting theory shows that traditional management accounting emphasizes cost reduction in which company-wide profit planning and budget management control the absolute value of costs at the manufacturing site. In other words, cost reduction in traditional management accounting theory is the management of financial figures.

3. Toyota Production System and Cost Reduction at Toyota

Ohno (1978), the founder of TPS, identified the following four aspects of the purpose of TPS: (1) TPS is a production method that enhances productivity by thoroughly eliminating all types of waste from companies. (2) Waste at the manufacturing site is an element of production that "increases only cost." For example, too many people, excess inventory, and excess equipment at the manufacturing site are wasteful. People, equipment, materials, and products that are additional to needs increase only the cost price. (3) Various types of secondary waste are derived due to waste at the manufacturing site. (4) TPS reduces the number of people and inventories, clarifies the surplus capacity of equipment, and eliminates secondary waste naturally by thoroughly eliminating waste. As a result, costs are reduced at manufacturing sites operated by TPS.

Ohno (1978) suggested the following basic ideas for thoroughly eliminating waste: (1) Improving productivity must ultimately lead to cost reduction. (2) Only necessary items must be made and by the minimum number of people. (3) Thorough elimination of waste must be promoted so that productivity can be improved, whether it is a single worker, a production line where workers are gathered, or the entire factory where production lines are gathered.

Ohno (1978) defined "working time" as "time to increase added value + wasted time." Improving productivity is to reduce wasteful time and raise the ratio of time to increase added value close to 100%. Therefore, in TPS, seven types of waste are thoroughly eliminated: (1) over-made waste, (2) waiting waste, (3) transportation waste, (4) processing waste, (5) inventory waste, (6) operation waste, and (7) defective product waste. By thoroughly eliminating these types of waste, work efficiency would be greatly improved. However, in TPS, it is not possible to make more than the required number, so if waste is thoroughly eliminated, the company would generate surplus personnel. In other words, TPS is a system that clarifies surplus personnel. The management must accurately grasp which personnel are surplus and make effective use of them. Meanwhile, for workers, if there is no wasteful work, the work will be more rewarding.

As mentioned above, Ohno (1978) argued that thoroughly eliminating waste would improve productivity. Thorough elimination of waste here is a voluntary and active kaizen activity by employees. In addition, thorough elimination of waste is a source of cost-reduction effects at manufacturing sites operated by TPS.

Next, Monden (2006) pointed out the following aspects of the purpose of TPS: (1) The ultimate purpose of a company is to generate profits. (2) TPS is an effective production method for companies to achieve their ultimate goals. (3) The basic goal of TPS is to improve productivity and reduce costs. (4) TPS thoroughly eliminates wasteful elements in production (excessive personnel, excessive inventory, etc.) through employee kaizen activities. (5) Kaizen activities eliminate various types of waste (hidden slack) in the company and reduce costs. As a result, businesses can earn a profit.

Monden (2006) presented the following route as a process by which waste increases costs: (1) Primary waste = excess people/excessive equipment (extra labor costs/extra depreciation costs) → (2) Secondary waste = over-made waste → (3) Tertiary waste = inventory waste (extra interest costs) → (4) Fourth waste = excessive warehouse, excessive transporter, excessive transportation equipment, excessive inventory manager, excessive quality maintainer, and excessive computer use (extra labor cost, extra depreciation costs). Meanwhile, Monden (2006) also presented the following two routes as a process by which TPS reduces costs: (1) Produce at selling speed (the central theme of TPS) → (2) Eliminate over-made waste → (3) Eliminate tertiary and fourth waste → (4) Reduce manufacturing overhead costs. (1) Produce at a selling speed (the central theme of TPS) → (2) Realize the waste of waiting time → (3) Reduce the number of people by redistributing work → (4) Reduce labor costs. The most important element here is the thorough elimination of excess labor and excess inventory. Kaizen activities carried out by employees at the TPS manufacturing site support this process.

The section provided an overview of cost reduction in Toyota's mass production process from the perspectives of Ohno (1978) and Monden (2006). From this, it can be seen that Toyota has adopted a unique form of cost reduction in its mass production process, which is primarily the management of activities, represented as follows: (1) At the manufacturing site operated by TPS, employees voluntarily and actively carry out kaizen activities. (2) Toyota collects the cost-reduction effect generated from employees' kaizen activities into the profit management system after the fact.

4. Respect for the Humanity of Employees

At the manufacturing site operated by TPS, employees voluntarily and proactively carry out kaizen activities to thoroughly eliminate waste, improve productivity, and as a result, reduce costs. Here, the main incentive for employees' voluntary kaizen activities is Toyota's value of respecting the humanity of employees.

Ohno (1978) pointed out that TPS is a system for fully utilizing the abilities of employees, enhancing their motivation to work, and performing work that eliminates waste completely.

Monden (2006) pointed out that the aims of TPS are to improve productivity and reduce costs without compromising the human dignity of employees. The conventional wisdom is that there are two ways to improve productivity: (1) reduce the labor force while maintaining the same production level and (2) produce more products with the existing labor force. Either way, an unacceptable sacrifice as a human being, that is, the loss of humanity of employees, is inevitable. However, at manufacturing sites operated by TPS, measures are taken to encourage employees to engage in voluntary kaizen activities through small group activities called QC circles. This solves the problem of conflict between productivity and humanity.

In QC circles, thorough elimination of waste is voluntarily promoted mainly as follows: (1) elimination of wasteful manual movements, (2) introduction of improved machines or new machines to avoid uneconomical use of human resources, (3) savings by changing the usage of materials and consumables, and (4) changing the machine layout to realize "one piece flow." Then, through the proposal system, award system, and profit management system, the cost-reduction effect generated by kaizen activities is systematically concentrated at the head office.

TPS can be said to be a system that maximizes the potential of employees through the voluntary execution of kaizen activities based on Toyota's value of respecting the humanity of employees (Figures 1–3).

5. Traditional Cost Reduction and Cost Reduction at Toyota

So far, we have reviewed the concepts of profit planning and budget management in management accounting theory, and considered traditional forms of cost reduction. In addition, based on previous research on TPS, we considered the cost reduction in Toyota's mass production process.

Figure 4 shows a conceptual diagram of traditional cost reduction, and Figure 5 shows a conceptual diagram of cost reduction in Toyota's mass production process. Based on these figures, the characteristics of Toyota-like cost management are clarified.

On the one hand, in traditional cost reduction, the company-wide profit plan formulated by the head office and the budget management

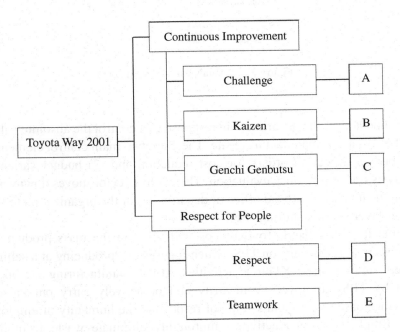

Figure 1. Toyota's Value System (1)

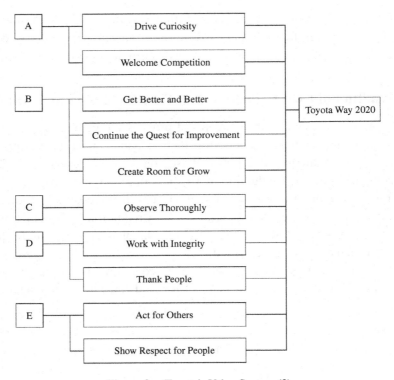

Figure 2.   Toyota's Value System (2)

implemented by the department in response to it control the absolute value of the cost at the manufacturing site. There are two main control elements: (1) budget execution orders for cost reduction and (2) budget variance analysis for performance evaluation. The control vector moves downward from the upper layer (head office or department) of the organization to the lower layer (manufacturing site).

On the other hand, Toyota's cost reduction in the mass production process mainly depends on TPS, which focuses on "producing at a selling speed" and includes QC circle activities. At the manufacturing site operated by TPS, employees voluntarily and proactively carry out kaizen activities based on Toyota's value of respecting the humanity of employees. Employee kaizen activities thoroughly eliminate waste from the manufacturing site, improve productivity, and produce cost-reduction effects. The generated cost-reduction effect amount is aggregated into the

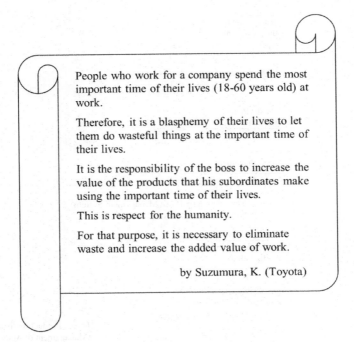

People who work for a company spend the most important time of their lives (18-60 years old) at work.

Therefore, it is a blasphemy of their lives to let them do wasteful things at the important time of their lives.

It is the responsibility of the boss to increase the value of the products that his subordinates make using the important time of their lives.

This is respect for the humanity.

For that purpose, it is necessary to eliminate waste and increase the added value of work.

by Suzumura, K. (Toyota)

Figure 3. Toyota's Respect for the Humanity

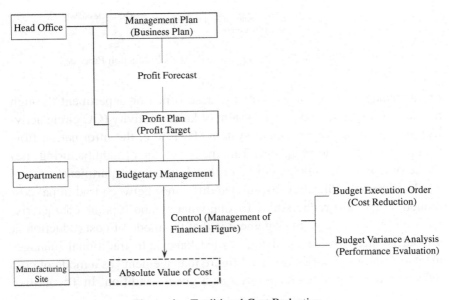

Figure 4. Traditional Cost Reduction

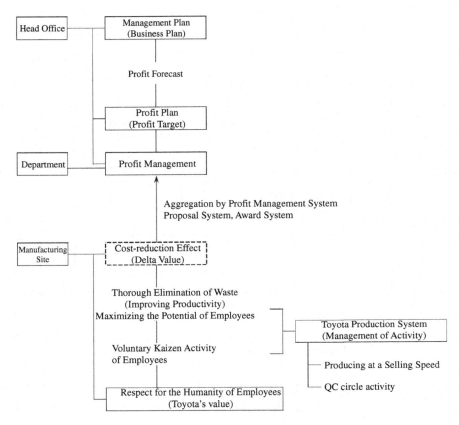

Figure 5.   Cost Reduction in Toyota's Mass Production Process

profit management framework of the head office or department through the proposal system and award system of kaizen activity (QC circle activity) and the profit management system. Therefore, the information flow vector in this case flows upward from the lower layer (manufacturing site) of the organization to the upper layer (head office or department).

In addition to the abovementioned difference between traditional cost reduction and cost reduction at Toyota, what symbolizes the characteristics of Toyota-like cost management is that the mode of cost reduction at Toyota is "activity management," called kaizen. In traditional management accounting theory, "financial figure management" as a mode of cost reduction has long been recognized as a given condition. In Toyota-like cost management, as presented in this chapter, the following two new aspects are included: (1) Cost reduction at the manufacturing site is achieved by "activity management" instead of "financial figure management" and (2) cost reduction by "activity management" is enabled by Toyota's value of respecting humanity.

The management accounting significance of such Toyota-like cost management is that it is possible to eliminate the harmful effects of controlling the absolute value of costs. According to Simons (1999), profit management systems generally face three risks: (1) setting a low target (arbitrarily set to increase the probability of achieving the target), (2) leveling business performance (forging transaction timing and records across accounting periods), and (3) information bias (report only good information and hide bad information). In Toyota-like cost management, the amount of cost-reduction effect generated from the voluntary kaizen activities of employees is aggregated in the profit management system after the fact. It becomes possible to eliminate it.

6. Conclusion

In this chapter, based on the concept of profit planning and budget management in management accounting theory and previous research on TPS, we compared the traditional type of cost reduction with the cost reduction in Toyota for the mass production process. Then, we clarified the characteristics of Toyota-like cost management and considered its significance in management accounting.

The Toyota-like cost management identified in this chapter is very different from the traditional management accounting theory, which requires "financial figure management" as a given condition, and has a unique aspect of cost reduction in "activity management" based on kaizen. In addition, a characteristic of Toyota-like cost management is that cost reduction by "activity management" is enabled by Toyota's value of respect for the humanity of employees.

The discussion in this chapter highlights the following issues for future research: (1) Is cost reduction in the form of "activity management" peculiar to TPS and Toyota, or are there similar cases? If so, in what kind of industry, region, and company does it occur, under what conditions, and in what form and content? Verification of the universality of the Toyota-like cost management concept is an issue for future research. (2) Would the accuracy of eliminating waste and improving productivity be further improved by utilizing digital technology? Examining the future evolution of Toyota-like cost management through digital transformation remains an issue for future research.

References

Dean, J. (1951). *Managerial Economics*. Prentice Hall, Inc., New Jersey.

Horngren, C. T., Sundem, G. L., Schatzberg, J. O., and Burgstahler, D. (1999). *Introduction to Management Accounting*, 11th ed., Prentice Hall, Inc., New Jersey.

Knoeppel, C. E. (1930). Wanted — The Profit Engineer. *Factory and Industrial Management*, January, 37–38.

Knoeppel, C. E. (1931). The Technique of the Profitgraph. *Factory and Industrial Management*, December, 789–791.

Monden, Y. (2006). *Toyota Production System: Its Theory and System*, Diamond, Inc., Tokyo (in Japanese).

Nishimura, A. and Oshita, J. (2007). *Basic Management Accounting*, Chuokeizai-Sha, Tokyo (in Japanese).

Ohno, T. (1978). *Toyota Production System: Beyond Large-Scale Production*, Diamond, Inc., Tokyo (in Japanese).

Okamoto, K., Obata, H., Hiromoto, T., and Hiki, F. (2003). *Management Accounting*, Chuokeizai-Sha, Tokyo (in Japanese).

Simon, H. A. (1960). *The New Science of Management Decision*, Harper & Brothers Publishers, New York.

Simons, R. (1999). *Performance Measurement and Control Systems for Implementing Strategy*, Prentice Hall, Inc., New Jersey.

Chapter 7

Study on Semiconductor Production Equipment Companies' ROESG Management

Soichiro Higashi

Chiba Institute of Technology, Chiba, Japan

1. Introduction

Recent years have witnessed a growing interest in how corporate managements' environment, social, and governance (ESG) strategies promote the long-term growth of their companies. The "Ito report" by the Ministry of Economy, Trade and Industry (a report from a Professor Kunio Ito-chaired study group that was published in August 2014) highlighted that companies' and investors' short termism, as well as the low profitability of Japanese companies, represent bottlenecks. The report estimated the average costs of shareholders' equities demanded by domestic and foreign institutional investors to be 7.2% (overseas) and 6.3% (domestic) and recommended the long-term enhancements of shareholder value by targeting the realization of an 8% return on equity (ROE), which would exceed these averages. Furthermore, Professor Ito proposed ROESG as a management model for reconciling companies' ROE and ESG, rather than regarding them as dichotomous opposites. One of Ito's efforts comprised the publication of the ROESG ranking as a comprehensive key performance indicator (KPI) for ROESG management. The ranking is calculated by first determining the three-period average of ROE, followed by multiplying the average by the ESG scores of five ESG evaluation organizations. In the second ROESG Ranking (FY2020 edition) by Nikkei Inc. and the QUICK ESG Research Institute, the semiconductor production equipment companies, Tokyo Electron Ltd. (TEL) and Advantest Corporation, ranked first and second in Japan, respectively, owing to their high capital efficiencies and proactive ESG initiatives.

Thus, this study focuses on the Japanese semiconductor production equipment companies that have demonstrated significant proactiveness toward achieving ROE and ESG by employing the ROESG ranking based on the "ROESG" model of Yanagi and Ito (2019), which presents a conceptual framework for synchronizing ROE and ESG. The results of the Toyo Keizai "CSR Survey: 16th Survey (2020 Survey)" will be utilized for ESG (non-financial information). Thereafter, to visualize the invisible value, correlation analysis was performed to elucidate the relationship between ESG and the price-to-book ratio (PBR), which is a function of ROE as a proxy variable for enterprise value.

2. Literature Review and Hypothesis Development

2.1 *Previous research on ROESG*

The General Pension Investment Fund (GPIF), which manages and invests the largest public funds globally, signed the Principles for Responsible Investment (PRI) in September 2015 and revised its investment principles, a promise to the public, in October 2017. It has strongly emphasized its commitment to promoting ESG-conscious investments in all assets, including stocks and bonds. As of December 2021, GPIF accounted for the management of more than 194 trillion yen, and the fund inflow to the stock market can significantly impact stock prices. Thus, their actions are attracting the attention of market participants. Consequently, the interest in and criticality of ESG (non-financial information) disclosure and elucidation are increasing daily, and ESG initiatives have emerged as urgent issues for companies. The extant studies on ROESG can be summarized as follows:

Lev and Gu (2016) observed that the explanatory powers of balance-sheet shareholders' equity and net income statement on the market capitalization of listed U.S. companies have reduced from 90% (the 1950s) to 50% (2013). Therefore, the value of financial information is subordinated to that of non-financial information in investors' investment decisions.

Ito (2021) believed that companies must construct and practice a management model that ensures sustainable corporate value creation by integrating high-level ROE and ESG management; he advocates "ROESG" management and encourages its practice by transcending the limitations and conflicts of the two management models (ROE and ESG). Among his efforts, Professor Ito's published ROESG Ranking, as a comprehensive KPI for ROESG management, has been implemented since 2019 under his supervision.

Yanagi and Ito (2019, p. 37) observed that the market value added (MVA = Market Value (MV) of equity – Book Value (BV) of equity) with a PBR of ≥1.0 is related to the ESG value (intrinsic value model) and correlates with the International Integrated Reporting Council (IIRC) five non-financial capital framework, namely the IIRC–PBR model (Figure 1). They presented a conceptual framework for synchronizing ESG and ROE based on the residual income model and proposed the integration of this relationship as the "ROESG" model.

Among the "ROESG" models, IIRC–PBR model integrates the BV of shareholders' equity (the PBR portion that is less than 1.0) with financial capital. MVA (the portion of PBR that is greater than 1.0) is associated with the five non-financial capitals (intellectual, human, manufactured, social and relationship, and natural capitals).

Based on this IIRC–PBR model, Tomizuka (2017) analyzed and score integrated the report descriptions of the Japanese healthcare sector and

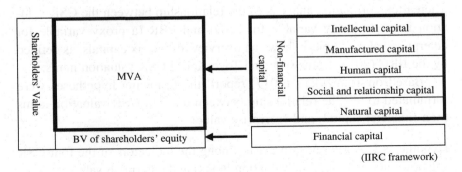

(IIRC framework)

Figure 1. IIRC–PBR Model, A Conceptual Framework of the "ROESG" Model

Source: Yanagi and Ito (2019, p. 37, Chart 1).

revealed a positive correlation between the five IIRC non-financial capitals and PBR. Yanagi and Ito (2019, pp. 37–38) revealed that this evidence supports the basic "ROESG" model.

2.2 *Hypothesis development*

The analytical method of this study was based on the IIRC–PBR model of Yanagi (2015), which is among the framework of the "ROESG" model of Yanagi and Ito (2019). The ROESG model presents the synchronization of ROE and ESG as its conceptual framework. Here, we adopted Tomizuka's (2017) method to elucidate the relationship between the non-financial capital and enterprise values of pharmaceutical companies.

PBR is interpreted as a function of ROE, since PBR = PER × ROE. The relationship between PBR and non-financial capital can be interpreted, as follows: a company with high PBR is assumed to possess a large equity spread; conversely, it can be interpreted as the market fully factoring in the value of non-financial capital (Yanagi, Meno, and Yoshino, 2016). Therefore, it is reasonable to select PBR as a proxy variable for enterprise value, as employed in the IIRC–PBR model among the "ROESG" models, because companies with PBR values of ≥1.0 may reflect certain non-financial information.

The analysis reported here targets Japanese semiconductor production equipment companies (six companies) listed on the stock market with a five-level rating (AAA, AA, A, B, and C) on all the corporate social responsibility (CSR) valuation items (human resources, environment (E), social (S), governance (G), and basics) in Toyo Keizai Inc. (2021a, 2021b). Thereafter, correlation analysis of the relationship between the CSR valuation items (a proxy variable for ESG) and PBR (a proxy variable for enterprise value). Table 1 shows an overview of the six capitals, as defined by the IIRC (2013) framework and Toyo Keizai CSR valuation items.

Based on Tomizuka's (2017) report, the following hypotheses were formulated to test the relationship between the four CSR valuation items (non-financial capital) and enterprise value:

Hypothesis 1: A relationship exists among the indicators of the four CSR valuation items (total CSR valuation items) and enterprise value.

Hypothesis 2: Human resources and ESG are related to enterprise value.

Table 1. Comparison of the Six Capital Outlines, as Defined by the IIRC (2013) Framework and Toyo Keizai CSR Valuation Items

IIRC (2013) Six Capitals		Outline	Toyo Keizai CSR Valuation Items	
Non-financial capital	Intellectual capital	Value of research and development (R&D), including intangible assets, such as patents and intellectual properties	—	Total CSR valuation items
	Human capital	Capabilities and experiences of personnel and their willingness to innovate	Human Resources	
	Manufactured capital	Facilities employed to manufacture products or deliver services	—	
	Social and relationship capital	Relationship between public trust and various stakeholders	S, G	
	Natural capital	Environmental resources and processes affected by corporate activities	E	
Financial capital		The financial basis supporting corporate activities, narrowly defined, the BV of shareholders' equity for accounting purposes	—	

3. Research Design

3.1 *Subject*

For this analysis, six companies were selected from the following Toyo Keizai Inc. (2021a, 2021b): DISCO Corporation, Advantest Corporation, Nikon Corporation, SCREEN Holdings Co. Ltd., Canon Inc., and TEL. Thus, the implications of this study are essentially applicable to semiconductor production equipment companies.

3.2 *Method*

To test the hypotheses, Tomizuka's (2017) analysis method was employed as a reference to evaluate the CSR valuation items (human resources and ESG) in Toyo Keizai Inc. (2021a, 2021b) for the sample companies, with each valuation item being numerically evaluated. For the enterprise value, PBR was employed as a proxy variable. The analysis procedure began with exploratory data analysis in which the relationship between CSR valuation items and PBR was examined with SPSS (SPSS Statistics 27). Next, for the confirmatory data analysis, only the non-financial information disclosures, which exhibited a positive relationship, as revealed by the exploratory data analysis, were extracted. Finally, the hypotheses were tested again by employing SPSS.

The CSR valuation items and the number of items (Toyo Keizai Inc., 2021a, 2021b) for each CSR valuation item in the exploratory data analysis are as follows: human resources (45), S (30), G (38), and E (30). For their quantification, they were rated as "1" and "0" if they were disclosed and undisclosed, respectively. Thereafter, the total CSR valuation items of each of the four CSR valuation items were calculated. Furthermore, the variables were manipulated to afford each CSR valuation item a maximum score of 25 points, thus ensuring that the total of the CSR valuation items for the analyzed companies was 100 points. Finally, the relationships between the scores of the disclosure content and PBR of each CSR valuation item and the total CSR valuation items, respectively, were examined, and this facilitated the exploration of the relationship between the disclosure content and PBR.

In the confirmatory data analysis, only the CSR valuation items for which the exploratory data analysis exhibited a positive correlation were extracted. The total value was further calculated with the extracted disclosure contents. Furthermore, the variables were manipulated to a maximum score of 25 points for each CSR valuation item so that the total of the CSR valuation items was 100 points for the surveyed companies. Finally, the relationships between the scores of the disclosure content and PBR of each CSR valuation item and the total of CSR valuation items, respectively, were reexamined.

4. Verification Results

4.1 *Exploratory data analysis*

Regarding the exploratory data analysis, Pearson's product–moment correlation coefficients were calculated to test the strength of the relationship between the CSR valuation items and PBR, and the results demonstrated that the relationships between the disclosure scores and PBR of each CSR valuation item and the total of CSR the valuation items were all negative correlations. The analysis of the descriptive statistics of the CSR valuation items and enterprise value (Table 2) revealed that the standard deviations of the CSR valuation items and PBR were small, although the standard deviation of the ROE of the former was larger. Three companies (Nikon Corporation, SCREEN Holdings Co. Ltd., and Canon Inc.) fell short of the ≥8.0% ROE, which was specified in the Ito Report of the Ministry of Economy, Trade and Industry (2014), with Nikon Corporation's ROE exhibiting a negative value. The PBRs of Nikon Corporation and Canon Inc. were <1.0; thus, they did not satisfy the assumption of the IIRC–PBR model in which companies with PBRs of ≥1.0 might reflect some non-financial information. Therefore, the three companies with ROEs of ≥8.0% and PBR of ≥1.0 (DISCO Corporation, Advantest Corporation, and TEL) as well as the three companies with ROEs of <8.0% or PBR of <1.0 (Nikon Corporation, SCREEN Holdings Co. Ltd., and Canon Inc.) were divided into two groups and subjected to another round of exploratory data analysis again.

In the exploratory data analysis, all the correlations for the two groups were positive except for S (Table 3). Although the group of firms with ROEs of ≥8.0% and PBR of ≥1.0 exhibited stronger positive correlations

Table 2. Descriptive Statistics for the CSR Valuation Items (Exploratory Data Analysis)

Valuation Items	Mean	S.D.	Min.	Med.	Max.	N
Enterprise value						
ROE	12.48	13.38	−6.40	12.17	27.27	6
PBR	3.77	2.93	0.71	3.58	7.18	6
Non-financial information						
CSR valuation items: 100-point evaluation						
Human resources	19.48	2.27	16.22	19.26	22.07	6
E	17.00	4.66	9.91	17.23	22.52	6
S	20.53	2.15	17.28	21.51	22.43	6
G	18.79	2.95	14.29	19.64	21.94	6
Total CSR valuation items	75.81	10.43	57.69	77.25	86.84	6

Table 3. Correlation of PBR and CSR Valuation Items (Exploratory Data Analysis)

	Human Capital	Natural Capital	Social and Relational Capital		Non-financial Capital	
	Human Resources	E	S	G	Total CSR Valuation Items	N
ROE of ≥8.0% and PBR of ≥1.0	0.950	0.968	0.818	0.542	0.985	3
ROE of <8.0% or PBR of <1.0	0.502	0.361	−0.955	0.924	0.333	3
Total of six companies	−0.424	−0.304	−0.314	−0.496	−0.419	6

than the group of firms with ROEs of <8.0% or PBR of <1.0, no significant positive correlations were observed at the 5% level. Among the group of firms with ROEs of ≥8.0% and PBR of ≥1.0, the positive correlation at the level of significance approached 10% for the total CSR valuation items; thus, confirmatory data analysis was performed for this group of firms.

4.2 *Confirmatory data analysis*

For the confirmatory data analysis, only the valuation contents with positive relationships were extracted from the exploratory data analysis results. The valuation items, which were extracted from the exploratory data analysis results are as follows (Tables 4 and 5).

The descriptive statistics for the CSR valuation items and enterprise value are presented in Table 6. The mean total of the CSR valuation items in non-financial capital was 71.83. The companies with the highest and lowest total CSR valuation items scored 83.11 and 52.91, respectively. The means were slightly lower than the statistics obtained from the exploratory data analysis, although they were quite constant. Conversely, the disparity in the scores between the companies increased probably because the extraction of the CSR valuation items significantly separated the companies that disclosed their CSR valuation items from those that did not. Additionally, the standard deviations of all the non-financial

Table 4. Valuation Items for the Confirmatory Non-financial Capitals (Human Resources and G)

Human Resources	G
Ratio of female employees	Management philosophy as the basis for achieving medium- to long-term improvements in corporate values
Number of female employees by generation	Existence or non-existence of a CSR department
Status of job leavers	Stakeholder engagement
Disclosure of the total annual working hours	Involvement of third parties in activity reporting
Overtime hours and pay	Existence or non-existence of a CSR department
Efforts to reduce overtime work	Presence or absence of a CSR officer
Average wage for 30-year-olds	Responsibilities of the CSR officer
Availability of foreign managers	Documentation of the CSR policy
Ratio of female managers	IR department
Percentage of female managers and higher ranks	Legal-compliance-related departments
Percentage of female executives	Participation in domestic and international CSR-related standards, etc.
Basic philosophy of diversity promotion	Availability of an internal audit department
Management policy of respecting diversity	Establishment of internal and external contact points for whistleblowing and reporting
Diverse human resources promotion department	Establishment of rules to protect the rights of whistleblowers and reporters
Targeted value of diverse managerial appointments	Disclosure of the number of whistleblowing and reporting
Employment rate of persons with disabilities (actual)	Cease and desist orders, etc. from the Fair Trade Commission, etc.
Target rate of employing persons with disabilities	Suspension of operations and businesses because of misconduct, etc.
Employment up to the age of 65	Criminal charges for compliance-related incidents and accidents
Percentage of paid leave taken	Caught in an overseas price cartel
Maternity leave	Exposed overseas bribery

(Continued)

Table 4. (*Continued*)

Human Resources	G
Employees taking childcare leave	Anticorruption and bribery policy
Male employees taking childcare leave	Disclosure of political contributions, etc.
Percentage of male employees taking childcare leave	Assessment of an internal control
Spouse maternity leave system	Disclosure on the status of the advisor and counsel system
Employees taking nursing care leave	Existence or non-existence of a security policy for information systems
Nursing care leave/nursing care leave	Privacy policy
Reemployment system for retired employees	Risk and crisis management structure
Occupational injury frequency	Basic policy on risk and crisis management
Number of employees on mental health leave	Availability of response manuals for risk and crisis management
Policy on respect for human rights, etc.	Head of the risk and crisis management system
Status of response in the four core labor standard areas	Business continuity management (BCM) construction
Disclosure of employee evaluation criteria	Business continuity planning (BCP) formulation
Disclosure of competence and evaluation results to the individual	Status of the risk and crisis management initiatives
Retention of new graduates	Documentation and disclosure of corporate ethics policies
Disclosure of labor issues that have arisen	Existence or non-existence of codes of ethical conduct, norms, and manuals

capitals increased in value, confirming the increased variability of the valuation scores.

For the confirmatory data analysis, Pearson's product–moment correlation coefficients were calculated again to verify the strength of the relationship between the CSR valuation items and PBR, and the results of the analysis are presented in Table 7. A strong positive correlation was

Table 5. Valuation Items for the Confirmatory Non-financial Capitals (E and S)

E	S
Existence or non-existence of a department in charge of the environment	Availability of consumer relations department
Presence or absence of an environment officer	Existence of a department in charge of social contribution
Responsibilities of an environment officer	Existence or non-existence of departments related to safety and safety systems for products and services
Availability of environmental policy documents	Expenditure on social contribution activities
Availability of accounting for environmental accounting	Cooperation with non-profit organizations (NPOs), non-governmental organizations (NGOs), etc.
Status of understanding the costs and benefits of accounting for the environment	Disclosure of ESG information
Disclosure of accounting for the environment	Dialogue with investors and ESG institutions
Performance disclosure status	Status of inclusion in ESG indexes, etc.
Implementation status of environmental auditing	Availability of manuals for responding to consumer complaints, etc.
ISO14001 acquisition system	Acquisition status of ISO9000S (domestic and overseas)
ISO14001 acquisition rate (domestic and overseas)	Achievements in community involvement activities
Green purchasing ratio of office supplies, etc.	Educational and academic support activities
Green procurement of raw materials	Cultural, artistic, and sports activities
Environmental labeling	International exchange activities
Assessing soil and groundwater contaminations	Implementation of CSR procurement
Awareness of water issues	Examples of CSR procurement initiatives
Existence or non-existence of the violations of environment-related laws and regulations	Basic policy for business partners

(*Continued*)

Table 5. *(Continued)*

E	S
Accidents or pollution that induce environmental issues	Conflict minerals
Existence or non-existence of a medium-term plan for reducing CO_2 emissions and other emissions in the environmental field	Volunteer leave
Scope 3	SDGs and targets
Environmental targets and achievements for fiscal 2019	BOP business initiatives
Initiatives for addressing climate change	Activities to solve problems overseas
Introduction of renewable energy	Pro bono support
Environment-related awards	CSR-related awards
Initiatives for conserving biodiversity	Reconstruction assistance for the Great East Japan Earthquake and other disasters
Expenditure on biodiversity conservation projects	

Table 6. Descriptive Statistics for the CSR Valuation Items (Confirmatory Data Analysis)

Valuation Items	Mean	S.D.	Min.	Med.	Max.	N
Enterprise value						
ROE	23.40	6.07	16.40	26.52	27.27	3
PBR	6.32	1.17	4.99	6.78	7.18	3
Non-financial information						
CSR valuation items: 100-point evaluation						
Human resources	19.76	5.37	13.57	22.50	23.21	3
E	14.68	5.20	9.05	15.71	19.29	3
S	19.36	2.50	16.92	19.23	21.92	3
G	18.02	4.39	13.37	18.60	22.09	3
Total CSR valuation items	71.83	16.48	52.91	79.46	83.11	3

Table 7. Correlation between PBR and the CSR Valuation Items (Confirmatory Data Analysis)

	Human Capital	Natural Capital	Social and Relational Capital	Non-financial Capital	
	Human Resources	E	S	G	Total CSR Valuation Items	N
ROE of ≥8.0% and PBR of ≥1.0	0.971	0.984	0.972	0.738	0.988*	3

Note: *$p < 0.05$.

observed at the 5% level for only the total CSR valuation items. Regarding the confirmatory data analysis based on the disclosure contents in which only the valuation items exhibiting a positive relationship were extracted from the results of the exploratory data analysis, it was assumed that the companies with higher scores on their total CSR valuation items might also account for higher enterprise values.

4.3 *Analysis results*

The calculation of the correlation coefficients for the confirmatory data analysis revealed that the correlation coefficient between the total CSR valuation items and PBR was 0.998 ($p < 0.05$). Thus, "Hypothesis 1: A relationship exists between the indicators of the four CSR valuation items (total CSR valuation items) and enterprise value" was supported. The human resources and ESG were insignificant. Therefore, "Hypothesis 2: Human resources and ESG are related with enterprise value" was rejected. Thus, the empirical research on the relationship between non-financial information and enterprise value, which was the objective of this study, partially clarified that the content of non-financial information disclosure impacts enterprise value.

5. Conclusion

This study indicated that the semiconductor production equipment companies in Japan with higher scores regarding their total CSR valuation items in the "CSR Survey" of Toyo Keizai out of the four CSR valuation items also exhibited higher enterprise values compared with those with lower scores. This finding indicated that the relationship between the content of non-financial information disclosure and enterprise value was clarified (although indirectly) via the IIRC framework (human, social and relational, and natural capitals), and the contribution of this study to the extant literature is to clarify the following two points:

(1)   As an alternative to the integrated report, this study quantified the content of the non-financial information disclosure in the results of the "CSR Survey" of Toyo Keizai and performed exploratory and confirmatory data analyses in succession. This series of analyses indicated that this process could be employed as a method for verifying the relationship between the content of non-financial information disclosures and enterprise value from outside the company.

(2)   A correlation analysis was performed to elucidate the relationship between the CSR valuation items and enterprise value (PBR) by dividing the surveyed companies (six companies) into two groups: "those with ROEs of $\geq 8.0\%$ and PBR of ≥ 1.0" (three companies) and "those with ROEs of $<8.0\%$ or PBR of <1.0" (three companies). This series of analyses indicated that this process could be employed as a method for verifying the relationship between the content of non-financial information disclosures and enterprise value from outside the company.

Since the analysis was limited to semiconductor production equipment companies, PBR, which was employed as a proxy variable for enterprise value, could not be calculated because some of the target companies were delisted owing to recent corporate restructuring, although they responded to the Toyo Keizai CSR Survey. The scope of future analyses would be expanded to the 33 industry categories on the Tokyo Stock Exchange to "visualize the invisible value" and further elucidate the usefulness of non-financial information.

References

International Integrated Reporting Council (IIRC) (2013). International Integrated Reporting Framework.

Ito, K. (2021). *Corporate Value Management*, Nikkei Business Publications, Inc. (in Japanese), Tokyo.

Lev, B. and Gu, F. (2016). *The End of Accounting and the Path Forward for Investors and Managers*, John Wiley & Sons (Translation supervised by Ito, K. (2018). *Accounting Rebirth: A Revolution for Investors and Managers in the 21st Century*, Chuokeizai-sha (in Japanese)), Tokyo.

Ministry of Economy, Trade and Industry (2014). Ito Report: Competitiveness and Incentives for Sustainable Growth: Building Desirable Relationships between Firms and Investors: Project (in Japanese).

Toyo Keizai Inc. (2021a). *CSR Company Directory (ESG Edition)*, Toyo Keizai Inc. (in Japanese), Tokyo.

Toyo Keizai Inc. (2021b). *CSR Company Directory (Employment and Human Resources Edition)*, Toyo Keizai Inc. (in Japanese), Tokyo.

Tomizuka, Y. (2017). Is Non-financial Capital Linked to Firm Value? — An Empirical Analysis Based on Integrated Reports of Pharmaceutical Companies, *Journal of Accounting*, **69**(7), 116–122 (in Japanese).

Yanagi, R. (2015). *Financial Strategy in the ROE Revolution*, Chuokeizai-sha (in Japanese), Tokyo.

Yanagi, R. and Ito, K. (2019). The ROESG Model and Evidence on Natural Capital, *Monthly Capital Markets*, **409**, 36–46 (in Japanese).

Yanagi, R., Meno, H., and Yoshino, T. (2016). Study of Synchronization Model of Non-financial Capital and Equity Spreads, *Monthly Capital Markets*, **2016**(11), 4–13 (in Japanese).

Chapter 8

Healthcare Organizations and Sustainability: Current Situations and Challenges

Aiko Kageyama

Hiroshima International University
Hiroshima, Japan

1. Introduction

In recent years, interest in sustainability has increased in many industries and organizations in Japan, and this philosophy has been incorporated into the management and day-to-day operations of organizations.

Currently, the world's shared sustainability goals are articulated in the Sustainable Development Goals (SDGs) adopted by the United Nations (UN) in 2015, which are to be achieved by 2030. Japan, as a member of an affiliated country, has been actively promoting SDGs.

The Japan SDG Action Platform, established by the Ministry of Foreign Affairs of Japan, presents annual SDG Awards to companies and organizations that demonstrate the best practices on SDG activities. These results have made it obvious that the SDGs are widely accepted regardless of industry and that many organizations are making an effort to achieve sustainable goals.

This study examines the appropriate understanding of sustainability in healthcare organizations (mainly hospitals and related facilities) in Japan. There has not yet been an accumulation of academic previous research on sustainability and related sustainable development in healthcare organizations, perhaps because the mission of healthcare organizations is related to people's health and lives, which are taken for granted as being sustainable. However, the actual situation and methods of development have not been discussed, and there are therefore many topics that should be considered for further research.

This study assumes that healthcare organizations are sustainable organizations based on their missions. First, we summarize the general concepts of sustainability, sustainable development, and sustainable (sustainability) management. Next, we present a brief survey on the SDGs in terms of the status of implementation of sustainable development in Japanese healthcare organizations. To learn from overseas, the case of the National Health Service (NHS) in the United Kingdom is referenced in this chapter.

Finally, this study will focus on the relationship with local communities and sustainability with healthcare organizations, and new issues are expected to be found for future research topics.

2. Sustainability and Sustainable Practices

2.1 *Conceptual framework for sustainability*

In Europe and the United States, the Industrial Revolution that began at the end of the 19th century gradually caused air pollution, soil contamination, and degradation of water quality. This economic and industrial development that progressed in developed countries from the 1960s to the 1970s made environmental problems more serious than ever.

Against this backdrop, the concept of sustainability has been subject to a variety of interpretations and definitions.

The common denominator is based on the concept of the entire earth being "a system connected in space and time" (Csorba and Rusu, 1992, p. 46), and sustainability should be continuously developed with the growth of the economy and society in the future based on environmental conservation in a finite resource environment. In other words, sustainability places a priority on the preservation of the natural environment (EPA, 2011, p. 15) and the optimal balance between the environment, society, and the economy (The UN, 1987).

2.2 Sustainable development

The concept of sustainable development is said to have originated at an international conference in 1972 in response to possible future environmental issues and the energy crisis (i.e., the oil crisis) that was occurring at the time (Csorba and Rusu, 1992, p. 47). The most widely used definition of sustainable management is found in the Report of the World Commission on Environment and Development: Our Common Future, commonly known as the Brundtland Commission Report, published by the UNs in 1987. It refers to "development that satisfies the needs of present generations while meeting the needs of future generations" and is "not a fixed state of harmony, but rather a variety of processes, including the exploitation of resources, the direction of investment, the application of technological innovations and organizational change, which are shared with the future as well as with present needs" (Ministry of Foreign Affairs HP). It refers to future-oriented activities that can be directed toward solving problems in the present as well as in the future.

Sustainable development has been changing over the years, and it is based on strategies that meet the needs of the following three pillars of the economy, environment, and society. It is being adapted to the different situations in various countries (Csorba and Rusu, 1992). When it comes to companies, needs are more individualized depending on the type of industry and size of the organization. Since the strategies to meet those needs differ, the three pillars of the environment, society, and economy should be different for each organization. The key here is to identify what the current "needs" are based on the environmental, social, and economic axes and then to identify who those "needs" are and what specific actions should be taken to address those needs.

2.3 Sustainable (sustainability) management

Sustainable (sustainability) management is also referred to as sustainability management and can be described in various ways, for example, as "management that seeks to improve the sustainability of business through consideration of environmental, social, and economic sustainability" (Mitsubishi, 2021), "management that allocates resources in order to continue to generate profits over the long-term" (PWC HP), or more simply, "management that takes into account social sustainability" (Nomura Research Institute HP).

Sustainable management is said to have originally been incorporated into management since the 2000s, as companies strive to "solve social issues such as environmental protection and achieve corporate growth" in the process of increasing corporate social responsibility (CSR), social contribution initiatives, and environmental social and governance (ESG) investment (IBM, 2018).

This sustainability management will impact society at large, and it is likely that various industries and business sectors will continue to consider how sustainability should be implemented and the methodology to improve it.

3. Healthcare Organization and Sustainability

3.1 *Perspectives on sustainability in Japanese healthcare organizations*

Sustainability in healthcare organizations has not been discussed enough in academic research and a different perspective then should be considered. In this era of declining birthrates and an aging population, the mission of the healthcare organization is closely related to the local community. In some places, they are the center of the community, so their sustainability should be examined not only as an independent organization but also as part of the entire community.

According to a document prepared by the Welfare and Medical Health Agency, there are two perspectives from which to consider sustainability in the management of a healthcare organization: the "aspects that ensure the effectiveness of future medical services" and "aspects related to finance and capital (or funding) base." The document also lists the following items for evaluating sustainability: "Does it meet local healthcare needs, healthcare policies, and local plans." The latter aspect is followed by an "analysis of income and expenditure and financial status from the viewpoint of business sustainability," which includes "whether the financial condition is being enhanced without damaging equity capital" in terms of profit and loss and "whether the company has the ability to pay debts that are coming due" in terms of cash flow. As can be seen from this, there is a way to maintain sustainability in a healthcare organization that emphasizes community relations in addition to the financial and capital aspects, which is an important part of building a sustainable society in the future.

3.2 *Examples of SDG initiatives at Japanese healthcare organizations*

The SDGs consist of 17 goals, as shown in Figure 1. In this section, we randomly selected seven healthcare organizations from the Internet to check the status of their efforts toward achieving the SDGs posted on their websites. The results are shown in Figure 2 (Kageyama, 2022).

As can be seen in Figure 1, it is clear that all hospitals are working on Goal 3 (health and welfare for all), Goal 4 (quality education for all), and Goal 8 (job satisfaction and economic growth), while none of them are involved in Goal 6 (safe water and toilets around the world). Goal 14 (protect the abundance of our oceans) is not applicable.

Figure 1. The 17 Goals of the SDGs Adopted by the UN

Source: Ministry of Foreign Affairs HP.

Organization/ SDGs	1	2	3	4	5	6	7	8	9	10	11	12	13	14	15	16	17
A Hospital Hokkaido	O		O	O				O		O	O					O	O
I Group Tokyo			O	O	O		O	O	O	O	O	O	O		O	O	O
K Center Ishikawa	O		O	O	O			O	O	O							
K Municipal Hospital, Nagoya			O	O	O			O	O	O	O		O		O	O	O
W kai Gifu			O	O	O			O			O	O	O				O
H Hospital Tottori			O	O				O			O	O					
K-kai Hiroshima	O	O	O	O	O			O			O	O	O		O	O	O
S Hospital Gunma	O	O	O	O	O			O			O	O	O				O

Figure 2.   Status of SDGs' Initiatives by Healthcare Organizations
Source: Kageyama (2022).

These organizations try to achieve the goals indicated with "O" in Figure 2, but in many cases, some goals are combined for one objective or activity so that the organizations widely cooperate and work together inside and outside with employees, patients, and local communities.

Goal 3 (health and welfare for all) of the SDGs is the very mission of healthcare organizations' work, and it is also a goal that all healthcare organizations are pursuing, which indicates that the SDGs provide another important management and activity framework for healthcare organizations.

3.3 *Sustainability in foreign healthcare organizations*

In foreign countries, when considering sustainability of a healthcare organization, healthcare organizations are recognized as being involved in two aspects of the industry: they are a main actor causing climate changes and they are also responsible for dealing with them.

In Europe and the United States, in particular, there is a tendency for environmental conservation activities to be fully emphasized to ensure sustainability (Deloitte, 2022). Therefore, sustainability is something that can be maintained by first aiming to protect and restore natural resources and then improve environmental pollution. This priority is reflected in the actual activities of each organization. Indeed, if we consider that the global healthcare industry is a single country, it would be the fifth-largest emitter of greenhouse gases in the world (Health care without harm, 2019), which is characterized by a concentration of energy consumption, food production, anesthetic gas use, transportation, etc., which are all carbon-related factors (carbon-intensive) (Deloitte, 2022).

Although this section does not discuss foreign healthcare organizations separately, the National Health Service (NHS), which oversees healthcare services in the United Kingdom, will also refer to the sustainability initiatives that it requires of its healthcare organizations.

NHS England published in 2014 its "2014–2020 Sustainable, Resilient, Healthy People and Places — A Strategy for Sustainable Development for the NHS, Public Health and the Care Social System;" the NHS has established an organizational plan for the future for all organizations under its jurisdiction (healthcare institutions, facilities, etc.) and has set three overarching goals. The first is the goal of making changes toward "A healthier environment" by contributing to the Climate Change Act's target of a 34% reduction in carbon emissions by 2020 in the United Kingdom. The second goal is to ensure that "Communities and services are ready and resilient for changing times and climates." Various disasters and climate change cause the worst damage when they strike helpless people and communities, but rather than trying to deal with each disaster individually or in isolation, the goal is to create a system in which multiple companies and communities can provide better solutions by means of local planning and guarantee mechanisms. The third goal is to take advantage of "Every opportunity contributes to healthy lives, healthy communities, and healthy environments." This is based on the idea that all contracts and decisions in the healthcare system should provide immediate and long-term benefits so that people become healthier and require less care.

The report states that a sustainable healthcare system is only possible if communities and people are able to provide support for independent and

Table 1.   The Transition from the Position to a More Sustainable Future

From	To
Health care as an institution-led service	Health and social care as a part of the community
Curative and fixing medical care	Early intervention and preventative care
Sickness	Health and well-being
Professional	Personal
Isolated and segregated	Integrated and in partnership
Buildings	Healing environments
Decision-making based on today's finances	An integrated value of the future which accounts for the impacts on society and nature
Single indicators and out-of-date measurements	Multiple scorecard information and in real time
Sustainability as an add-on	Integration in culture, practice, and training
Waste and overuse of all resources	A balanced use of resources where waste becomes a resource
Nobody's business	Everyone's business

Source: NHS (2014, p. 8).

self-managed conditions, and that healthcare systems provide quality care and public healthcare without depleting natural resources and causing serious environmental damage. In addition, the report provides specific examples of how the sustainable future would be different from the current situation, as shown in Table 1, and lists the following five areas as national strategies focus on:

- leadership, participation, and development,
- healthy, sustainable, resilient communities,
- sustainable health and care models,
- commissioning and procurement,
- high carbon emission locations.

In the appendix of its annual report, it includes an assessment aligned to the SDGs. The specific activities for the applicable goals are almost exclusively related to the efficient use of natural resources and energy.

Other efforts are being undertaken that will lead to the health of the community as a whole, with clearly defined priorities.

4. Healthcare Organizations and Local Communities in Japan

4.1 *Role of healthcare organizations in local communities*

As discussed in Section 3 of this chapter, in the United Kingdom, healthcare organizations and facilities place importance on their ties to the community from the viewpoint of sustainability.

In Japan, the coronavirus disease 2019 disaster increased the significance of the presence of healthcare organizations in local communities. The healthcare supply system that is needed in each community was established, which certainly has a role to play in providing local healthcare. The continuation of the local provision of healthcare services also creates employment opportunities and has a ripple effect on local economic activities, such as employing many professional and non-licensed staff, giving back to the community through salary payments, and bringing revenue to local businesses when facilities are newly built, renovated, or repaired (Japanese Society of Rural Medicine, 2018).

Thus, healthcare organizations play an important role in many aspects, even in small regions. As the size of the institution grows, it also can have various impacts beyond the prefectural boundaries, becoming a core player again in employment and regional revitalization (Sakaguchi and Mori, 2018).

In Japan's rural areas, it is said that "healthcare and nursing care have a certain effect on regional development" and that "healthcare and nursing care are only superstructures built on communities" and in particular, "small and medium-sized hospitals in rural areas are sometimes said to be 'destined for the community'" (Nippon Igaku Shinpo, 2015).

Therefore, healthcare organizations have an impact on the local community and are considered to be entities that coexist with the community.

However, while pointing out that healthcare is an important infrastructure that supports and contributes to the region, some argue that it is difficult to have an image of regional development with healthcare as a core industry in the general public (Sakaguchi and Mori, 2018, p. 3).

4.2 *Sustainability in healthcare and nursing care in relation to the community*

Sustainability in the United Kingdom's healthcare environment focuses on the protection of natural resources as a strategy and provides a positive and concrete direction for making the entire community healthier.

Sustainability in the Japanese healthcare environment also features the common need to protect and increase natural resources in consideration of environmental conservation on this planet. As mentioned already, healthcare organizations could play a part in regional development, employment, and urban planning, and they coexist with the community as an essential part of the community, so sustainability should be considered not only for individuals or healthcare organizations but also for the local community as a whole.

In Japan, an example of how sustainability is related to the community is the integration of the SDGs and the community-based comprehensive care system.

WAKO Kai in Gifu Prefecture is a group of 1,600 employees that provide community healthcare, nursing care, welfare, disability, and childcare services. WAKO Kai has been working on the SDGs in full scale since 2020 in conjunction with the existing community comprehensive care system, focusing particularly on Goals 3, 4, 5, 8, 11, 12, 13, and 17. The method is to assign departments within the organization to be in charge of these goals and, from there, take action to achieve the goals by concretizing initiatives and sharing activities with each category (Table 2).

By 2030, WAKO Kai will have established issue categories that combine the above eight goals and address each issue as "contributing to the realization of a sustainable, smile-filled future society together with the local community" (Wako-kai, 2020).

5. Conclusion

5.1 *Summary*

In examining sustainability in healthcare organizations, in Japan, the concept is gradually introduced into the sector as some of them are already beginning to work along the SDGs and also appeal their activeness to the

Table 2. Examples of SDG Initiatives by the WAKO Kai Group

Issue Category	Examples of Initiative
Medical, nursing care, and welfare services	Augmenting the community comprehensive care system and improving the overall strength of medical care and welfare.
Environmental and resource measures	Food circulation within the group (dealing with food loss), support for vaccines by collecting plastic bottle caps, use of LED lighting, and promotion of purchasing products compliant with the Eco Mark and Green Purchasing Law.
Health management	Contributing to the development of systems and programs that enable diverse work styles and promote the health of the employees themselves, Kasu Ki, and the community.
Human resource development	Nurturing children's zest for life through the operation of certified childcare centers; career development of staff; promotion and development of employment of seniors, foreign nationals, and persons with disabilities; and the identification and development of nursing care personnel.
Contributing to the community	Proactive efforts to "community building" by holding classes to prevent nursing care, dementia, and frailty, organizing community cleanups and festivals, organizing community events for employees, and active participation in community events by employees. Realization of a community where no one is left behind.

Source: Wako Kai PDF document.

public through Web pages. However, there is no organization or group that leads or coordinates SDG efforts to promote sustainable management for sustainable communities or the world.

At this point in time, there are active efforts to apply the SDG framework to existing systems, such as the WAKO Kai, and although it is not a prominent trend, some hospitals are working to protect the environment, while others are deepening their relationship with the community through healthcare services and proactively building community.

A report issued by the NHS in the United Kingdom reveals that the emphasis for improving the sustainability of healthcare organizations is to engage in environmental conservation and that the emphasis is on integrating with the community in providing medical and nursing care services.

Since Japanese healthcare organizations have strong ties with local communities, the United Kingdom's efforts to improve sustainability by integrating with local communities will be a very helpful sample in future implementation.

5.2 *Issues related to sustainability in Japanese healthcare organizations*

Even though Japanese healthcare organizations share their mission as providing healthcare, they operate their management in different ways depending on establishment status and available financial resources. Also, the scale of presence of healthcare organizations in the community is not uniform, and there are various needs for now and future. However, without identifying those needs and priorities, their challenges to make people and community healthier would fail with low incentive. In addition, in Japan, the healthcare organizations do not disclose that their activities create serious environmental issues and now much promotion of sustainable management or discussing sustainability has not been proceeded yet. Healthcare organizations are not proactive in disclosing the necessary information for balanced development in the three areas of the environment, society, and economy. In this situation, it may not be easy to evaluate sustainability in each area.

5.3 *Research issues*

This study mainly used the SDGs' framework when considering sustainability in healthcare organizations. It was also possible to classify sustainability into environmental, social, and economic elements and consider sustainability in terms of all resources, such as natural capital (forests, fishery resources, mineral resources, ecosystem services, etc.), human capital (education, health, etc.), and man-made capital (equipment, machinery, buildings, roads, etc.) (Managi, 2022), and assign the SDGs to each type of capital for consideration.

In addition, it was possible to identify the relevant needs of healthcare organizations considering the characteristics of the region, the characteristics of the establishment (e.g., according to the classification of private or public hospitals, medical corporations, or social medical corporations, as defined by law), and the size, and identify how sustainability should be discussed and the objectives based on industry and organizational priorities.

Based on examples from overseas in which progress has already been made, it will be necessary to organize the methods of evaluating sustainability in healthcare organizations for future reference.

Many research issues are found through this study; however, it will be attained more interesting and enriching results with surveying overall healthcare organizations' SDGs or sustainable management, which is the next research target in the near future.

References

Committee on Incorporating Sustainability in the U.S. Environmental Protection Agency (2011). Sustainability and the U.S. EPA.

Csorba, L. M. and S. Rusu. (1992). The History of Sustainable Management — A Literature Review, Journal of Economics and Business Research, Volume XXI, No. 2, pp. 45–64.

Deloitte (2022). Sustainability in Healthcare. Two Sides of the Same Coin. https://www2.deloitte.com/ch/en/pages/public-sector/articles/sustainability-in-healthcare.html (viewed July 31, 2022).

Health Care without Harm. Health Care's Climate Footprint. How the Health Sector Contributes to the Global Climate Crisis and Opportunities for Action. Climate-smart health care series Green Paper Number One Produced in collaboration with Arup September 2019.

IBM (IBM Corporation) (2021). https://www.ibm.com/blogs/smarter-business/business/sustainable-management2021/ (in Japanese) (viewed September 1, 2022).

Japan Society of Rural Medicine (2018). Main Symposium: The Role of Community Medicine in Revitalizing the Community, *Journal of Rural Medicine*, **66**(6), 670–677 (in Japanese).

Japan SDGs Action Platform, Ministry of Foreign Affairs of Japan, https://www.mofa.go.jp/mofaj/gaiko/oda/sdgs/index.html (in Japanese) (viewed September 1, 2022).

Kageyama, A. (2022). The Sustainability of the Health Industry in Japan — Comparison of SDG Settings among Hospitals, *International Review of Business*, (22), 65–74, the Society of Business Administration, Kwansei Gakuin University, Japan.

Managi, S. (2022). Nikkei SDG/ESG Conference: ESG and Corporate Choices at a Crossroads, Panel Discussion 'Non-financial Information Disclosure to Reach Stakeholders,' material slides (in Japanese).

Mitsubishi (2021). Surviving Uncertain Times through Sustainability Management, https://www.mri.co.jp/knowledge/column/20200428.html (in Japanese) (viewed September 1, 2022).

National Health Services (2014). Sustainable, Resilient, Healthy People and Places — A Sustainable Development Strategy for the NHS, Public Health and Social Care System (2014–2020)s.

National Health Services (2019). Sustainable Development Management Plan (2019–2022).

National Health Services (2021). Sustainability Annual Report 2020–2021.

Nippon Igaku Shimpo (2015). Medical Care and Long-Term Care in Regional Development: Effective in Providing Employment and Promoting Social Participation? — From the Public Symposium of Medical Economics Forum Japan, *Weekly Nippon Igaku Shimpo*, No. 4776, p. 14 (in Japanese).

Nomura Research Institute, https://www.nri.com/jp/sustainability (viewed September 1, 2022)

Sakaguchi, K. and Mori, K. (2018). Regional Revitalization through Medical Care: A Case Study for Hypothesis Building, Nichi-Medical Research Institute Working Paper, No. 411 (in Japanese).

United Nations (1987). Report of the World Commission on Environment and Development: Our Common Future.

WAKO Kai Group (2020). Smile WAKO Kai 2030 Initiative Document. https://www.pref.gifu.lg.jp/uploaded/attachment/204404.pdf (in Japanese) (viewed September 1, 2022).

Chapter 9

Diversity Management Outcomes: Quantitative Verification of the Climate for Inclusion in the Japanese Hotel Industry

**Misato Tanaka*, Yuri Fukaya*, Runa Tsushima*,
Miyabi Nashiba*, Ayuko Komura†, and Kenichi Suzuki***

*Meiji University, Tokyo, Japan
†Kanagawa University, Kanagawa, Japan

1. Background and Purpose of the Study

In recent years, diversity management has been promoted among Japanese companies. Diversity management is defined as a comprehensive management process for creating an environment that works effectively for all employees (Thomas, 1991). The construct of diversity management is classified into two categories: one targeting superficial diversity (demographic), such as gender, race, and age, and the other targeting more in-depth diversity (attitudinal), such as work histories, attitudes, habits, and skill levels (Harrison, Price, and Bell, 1998). In Japanese firms, in particular, gender diversity management (GDM) efforts to promote women's activities are the most common (Waki, 2019; Nakamura, 2018). Behind this is the economic perspective of the need to cover labor shortages due to a declining birthrate and aging population through the continuous employment of women (Nakamura, 2017), and the ethical perspective of eliminating the disadvantaged position of women in the workforce (Gender Equality Bureau, Cabinet Office, Government of Japan, 2021). In the Gender Gap Index published by the World Economic Forum in March 2021, Japan is ranked 120th out of 156 countries, representing the lowest level among developed countries, suggesting that efforts to promote women's activities are a major issue for Japanese companies (Gender Equality Bureau, Cabinet Office, Government of Japan, 2021). However, few quantitative studies have examined the relationship between diversity management and its outcomes using a Japanese firm as a case study (Hotta, 2015).

Diversity management research overseas has focused on the concept of developing the "climate for inclusion," linking employee diversity in terms of gender, race, and nationality to results. The climate for inclusion is defined as an environment in which individuals of all backgrounds are treated fairly, valued for who they are, and can participate in decision-making (Nishii, 2013). The climate for inclusion has been demonstrated as necessary for diversity management to increase job satisfaction and commitment (Nishii, 2013; Mor Barak *et al.*, 2016). However, no studies have focused on the aspect of gender in diversity management or demonstrated the impact of GDM on organizational outcomes mediated by the climate for inclusion in Japanese firms. We hypothesize that incorporating the climate for inclusion into the model as a mediating variable between GDM and organizational outcomes could solve the problem of inconsistent effects between GDM and organizational outcomes.

This study examines whether GDM can enhance organizational outcomes through the mediating variable of the climate for inclusion, using the research site of Company A in the hotel industry, which has strategically implemented GDM for 16 years and achieved results.

The structure of this chapter is as follows: Section 2 outlines the hypotheses. Section 3 describes the analytical methods used to test the hypotheses, and Section 4 presents the results of the structural equation modeling (SEM). Section 5 closes this paper with a discussion regarding the significance of the study, remaining issues, and conclusions.

2. Hypotheses Setting

2.1 *Gender diversity management and the climate for inclusion*

The most prominent form of diversity management in Japan is GDM (Waki, 2019; Nakamura, 2018). It is clear that companies that prioritize making it easy for female employees to work leverage organizational management and team building to take advantage of the respective characteristics of men and women, making it easy for both male and female employees to work (Okubo, 2014).

Brimhall, Lizano, and Mor Barak (2014) found that establishing an environment that did not discriminate based on gender, age, or race increases employees' positive perceptions of their work environment and enhances the climate for inclusion.

Here, the climate for inclusion, as previously noted, is an environment in which individuals of all backgrounds are treated fairly, valued for who they are, and can participate in important decision-making (Nishii, 2013). This concept consists of three sub-concepts: (1) equitable employment practices, (2) integration of differences, and (3) inclusion in decision-making. Equitable employment practices refer to the establishment of a fair employment and benefits system within the organization that helps eliminate bias. The integration of differences is a concept that captures the inclusion of interpersonal relationships among diverse employees in the workplace. Integration of interpersonal relationships indicates that there is no discrimination based on race, gender, age, or other differences. The implementation of GDM will provide opportunities for both men and women to have active roles, regardless of gender, thereby ensuring fair personnel practices, eliminating gender discrimination, and promoting respect for all opinions. This will work toward eliminating discrimination between men and women and increase overall perception of the climate for inclusion, where people feel that their opinions are respected.

Based on Brimhall, Lizano, and Mor Barak (2014), the following hypothesis is proposed:

Hypothesis 1: Gender diversity management has a positive and significant impact on employee perceptions of the climate for inclusion.

2.2 *Relationship between the climate for inclusion and engagement*

Brimhall (2019) quantitatively demonstrated that in organizations that foster the climate for inclusion, employees' commitment to the organization increases, as they feel valued as important members of the organization. Commitment is a concept that "refers to attachment to or unity with the organization, or internalization of management philosophy, organizational culture, or organizational values" (Suzuki, 2013, p. 70), without considering employees' willingness to contribute (i.e., whether they are working voluntarily or intrinsically). Therefore, from the perspective of emphasizing intrinsic motivation, the concept of engagement has been used in the field of human resource management (Downey *et al.*, 2015). Here, engagement refers to "a positive, fulfilling, work-related state of mind that is characterized by vigor, dedication, and absorption" (Schaufeli *et al.*, 2002, p. 74).

It has been demonstrated in the field that highly engaged employees have a higher willingness to act voluntarily toward advancing organizational goals, and approaches to management that increase employee engagement have been attracting attention (Okada and Yoshida, 2019). Therefore, in this paper, we use the concept of engagement rather than commitment as the construct to describe employees' positive attitude toward the organization.

Organizations that foster the climate for inclusion, equal employment and benefits, the absence of discrimination, and an environment in which one's opinions are actively accepted are expected to increase employee engagement by making employees feel valued as important members of the organization. Therefore, the following hypothesis is proposed:

Hypothesis 2: A perceived climate for inclusion has a positive and significant impact on engagement.

2.3 *The indirect impact of gender diversity management on engagement through perceptions of the climate for inclusion*

Goswami and Goswami (2018) empirically show that gender, cultural, and ethnic diversity management in the workplace fosters the climate for inclusion, and such a climate increases employee engagement. Therefore, we set the following hypotheses:

Hypothesis 3: A perception of climate for inclusion mediates the relationship between gender diversity management and engagement.

2.4 *Relationship between engagement and turnover intention*

It has been demonstrated that the more engaged an employee is at work, the higher the employee's job retention intentions, leading to higher job satisfaction and performance and lower job change and turnover intention (Bakker *et al.*, 2008; Kim, Shin, and Swanger, 2009; Saks, 2006; Schaufeli and Bakker, 2004). Based on the above discussion, we propose the following hypothesis:

Hypothesis 4: Engagement has a significant negative effect on turnover intention.

3. Analysis Method

3.1 *Research site and data*

The reason for selecting Company A as the research site is that it is a leading-edge company that engages in a number of diversity management initiatives with the aim of becoming a company for which a diverse workforce can work regardless of gender, age, or disability. Specifically, the company is working to support women's careers by enhancing its maternity leave system, supporting women's return to work after marriage, and introducing a flextime system, including shorter working hours. The company has received several diversity management awards in recognition of its commitment to such activities.

Another decisive factor in the choice of research site is the significantly lower turnover rate compared to other hotel enterprises since the turnover rate of full-time employees at Company A is approximately in the low 9% range (in 2016).

Data were obtained from an employee satisfaction survey conducted in 2015, which was administered by means of a mailed questionnaire.

A five-point Likert scale was used for the question options: 1 = disagree, 2 = not really agree, 3 = neither agree nor disagree, 4 = somewhat agree, and 5 = agree. The number of valid responses was 5,388.

The characteristics of the sample are as follows: Gender distribution is 48.20% male and 44.30% female, and 66.10% of the respondents are in positions other than management. The percentage of employees whose first choice is Company A is 30.2%. The attributes of the respondents include 31.2% non-regular employees and 59.4% regular employees, and as to age, 2.7% are under 20, 29.10% are in their 20s, 22.50% are in their 30s, 20.40% are in their 40s, 13.20% are in their 50s, and 10.40% are 60 or older. The number of years of service is 18.30% in the first year, 19.50% for 2–3 years, 14.50% for 4–5 years, 22.90% for 6–10 years, 14.30% for 11–15 years, and 7.90% for 16 years or more.

3.2 *Measurements*

As described in the hypotheses discussion, variables of GDM, a perception of climate for inclusion, engagement, and turnover intention are used in this study. The questionnaires used for each of the measurement scales and their descriptive statistics are presented in Table 1. These questionnaires were designed through a series of meetings with three employees in Company A's Corporate Planning Department while referring to the statements of previous studies.

GDM was measured examining three questionnaire items: "Do you think the company allows women to continue working after marriage?" "Do you think the company allows employees to continue working after childbirth?" and "Do you think the company allows men and women to work equally?" The Cronbach's Alpha was 0.860.

The degree of perception of the climate for inclusion by employees (hereafter referred to as "perception of the climate for inclusion") was developed referencing Nishii's (2013) three sub-concepts of equitable employment practices, integration of differences, and inclusion in decision-making. The Cronbach's Alpha was 0.683.

Engagement was measured using a three-component questionnaire item to assess vigor, dedication, and absorption, referencing Schaufeli *et al.* (2002). Cronbach's Alpha was 0.840.

Table 1. Descriptive Statistics

Variables	Questions	Mean	S.D.
(1) GDM	Do you think the company allows women to continue working after marriage?	3.55	1.15
	Do you think the company allows employees to continue working after childbirth?	3.47	1.17
	Do you think the company allows men and women to work equally?	3.88	1.03
(2) Climate for inclusion	Do you think the system of promotion and advancement is fair?	3.50	1.11
	Do you think the company cares about each and every employee?	3.44	1.12
	Will your judgment be respected on the job?	3.78	0.99
(3) Engagement	Are there times when you are so absorbed in your current job that you lose track of time?	3.80	1.13
	Do you feel that your current job is challenging and fulfilling?	3.82	1.03
	Are you constantly improving the quality of your work?	4.08	0.82
(4) Turnover intention	Do you want to leave the company?	2.36	1.29
	Do you want to change jobs?	2.37	1.32

Turnover intention was defined as "an employee's willingness or desire to leave the organization" (Thoresen *et al.*, 2003, p. 918), as measured by two items referencing the measurement scales proposed by Laczo and Hanish (1999) and Hwang and Hopkins (2012). Cronbach's Alpha was 0.931.

Control variables included tenure (1: 1st year, 2: 2–3 years, 3: 4–5 years, 4: 6–10 years, 5: 11–15 years, and 6: 16 years or more); position (0: other than management and 1: management); age (1: under 20 years, 2: 20s, 3: 30s, 4: 40s, 5: 50s, and 6: 60s or more); gender (0: female and 1: male); the first choice (1: first choice, 2: semi-preferred, and 3: other); and attributes (0: non-regular employee and 1: regular employee).

4. Results

4.1 *Confirmatory factor analysis and Harman's single factor test*

First, a confirmatory factor analysis applying the maximum likelihood method was conducted using IBM AMOS 27.0, including goodness-of-fit index (GFI), adjusted goodness-of-fit index (AGFI), normed fit index (NFI), comparative fit index (CFI), and root mean square error of approximation (RMSEA). The goodness-of-fit indices were $\chi^2 = 1{,}571.835$, $df = 38$, GFI = 0.922, AGFI = 0.865, NFI = 0.933, CFI = 0.935, and RMSEA = 0.112. GFI, NFI, and CFI are considered to be a good fit when they are more than 0.90, and AGFI more than 0.85 (Komatsu, 2007). An RMSEA of 0.08 or less is desirable (Kline, 2015). The results of the analysis elicited good values for GFI, AGFI, NFI, CFI, and RMSEA, although not good levels, and verification proceeded using these data.

In addition, since all constructs in this analysis were collected from the same sample, common method bias was tested, using Harman's single-factor test (Harman, 1967). The results of the analysis showed that the one-factor model had $\chi^2 = 10{,}266.74$, $df = 44$, GFI = 0.638, CFI = 0.564, and RMSEA = 0.269, and the four-factor model described above was a better fit. Subsequently, the four-factor model was adopted to conduct the analysis. Table 2 presents the correlation matrix among the factors used in this analysis.

4.2 *Results of structural equation modeling (SEM)*

To test the hypotheses, a structural equation modeling (SEM) was conducted using IBM AMOS 27.0. The results of the analysis are shown in Figure 1.

Table 2.   Correlation Matrix

	(1)	**(2)**	**(3)**	**(4)**
(1) GDM	—			
(2) climate for inclusion	0.651**	—		
(3) engagement	0.459**	0.602**	—	
(4) turnover intention	−0.348**	−0.404**	−0.515**	—

Note: **$p < 0.01$

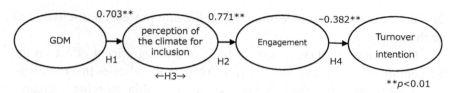

Figure 1. Results of Covariance Structure Analysis

Table 3. Tests for Indirect Effects Using Bootstrap Method (5,000 Repeated Samplings)

Independent Variable	Mediator	Dependent Variable	Estimated Value	Confidence Intervals	
				BCUL	BCLL
GDM	Perception of the climate for inclusion	Engagement	0.542***	0.602	0.485

Note: ***$p < .001$

First, GDM had a positive and significant impact on the perception of climate for inclusion. Hypothesis 1 was supported. Second, the perception of climate for inclusion increased engagement. Hypothesis 2 was supported.

The mediating relationship of the perception of climate for inclusion between GDM and engagement was estimated by testing for conditional indirect effects using the bootstrap method. The results of the indirect effects are presented in Table 3 (5,000 repeated samplings). As demonstrated, the indirect effect from GDM on engagement through the perception of climate for inclusion was positively significant, with lower and upper bounds of the 95% bias-corrected confidence interval for the estimate excluding zero ($\beta = 0.542$, $p < 0.001$, 95% confidence interval [0.485, 0.602]); thus, Hypothesis 3 was confirmed.

Regarding the relationship between engagement and turnover intention, Hypothesis 4 was supported, as engagement was determined to have a negative impact on turnover intention.

5. Discussion and Conclusion

The analyses in this paper assumed that the implementation of GDM increases engagement through the perception of the climate for inclusion and decreases turnover intention. The following presents a discussion of each hypothesis.

First, we find GDM to have a positive and significant effect on the perception of the climate for inclusion. This result indicates that establishing a workplace in which women are comfortable working increases employees' positive perceptions of the work environment, which engenders perceptions of the climate for inclusion.

Second, the climate for inclusion has a positive and significant impact on engagement. The results demonstrate that the climate for inclusion has a significant impact on engagement, which is considered to be more voluntary in nature and indicates a higher level of willingness to contribute to the company.

Third, the perception of the climate for inclusion is found to have a meditating relationship between GDM and engagement. It is suggesting the importance of the climate for inclusion for enhancing engagement through GDM.

Fourth, the results show that the effect of engagement on turnover intention is negatively significant, which is consistent with studies demonstrating that employees who are more engaged in their jobs have higher job retention, leading to lower intentions to change jobs or leave (Bakker *et al.*, 2008; Kim, Shin, and Swanger, 2009; Saks, 2006; Schaufeli and Bakker, 2004).

The significant contribution of this study fills a gap in the literature by investigating the effect of GDM on employee attitudes in a Japanese firm (Magoshi and Chang, 2009). The results indicate that the climate for inclusion and engagement are variables that explain the mechanism of the effect of GDM on turnover intention.

Future research issues are as follows:

First, it is expected that the model used in this study can be further generalized by verifying whether similar results can be obtained in other countries, industries, and companies in other sectors.

Second, it must demonstrate the usefulness of GDM more broadly by examining its impact not only on turnover intention but also on financial outcomes.

References

Bakker, A. B., Schaufeli, W. B., Leiter, M. P., and Taris, T. W. (2008). Work Engagement: An Emerging Concept in Occupational Health Psychology, *Work and Stress*, **22**(3), 187–200.

Brimhall, K. C. (2019). Inclusion and Commitment as Key Pathways between Leadership and Nonprofit Performance, *Nonprofit Management and Leadership*, **30**(1), 31–49.

Brimhall, K. C., Lizano, E. L., and Barak, M. E. M. (2014). The Mediating Role of Inclusion: A Longitudinal Study of the Effects of Leader–Member Exchange and Diversity Climate on Job Satisfaction and Intention to Leave among Child Welfare Workers, *Children and Youth Services Review*, **40**, 79–88.

Downey, S. N., Werff, L., Thomas, K. M., and Plaut, V. C. (2015). The Role of Diversity Practices and Inclusion in Promoting Trust and Employee Engagement, *Journal of Applied Social Psychology*, **45**(1), 35–44.

Gender Equality Bureau, Cabinet Office. (2021). *Kyodo-Partnership*, Gender Equality Bureau, Cabinet Office, May (in Japanese).

Goswami, S. and Goswami, B. K. (2018). Exploring the Relationship between Workforce Diversity, Inclusion and Employee Engagement, *Drishtikon: A Management Journal*, **9**(1), 65–89.

Harman, H. H. (1967). *Modern Factor Analysis*, University of Chicago Press, Chicago.

Harrison, D. A., Price, K. H., and Bell, M. P. (1998). Beyond Relational Demography: Time and the Effects of Surface- and Deep-Level Diversity on Work Group Cohesion, *Academy of Management Journal*, **41**(1), 96–107.

Hotta, A. (2015). A Study on the Future of Diversity Management Research in Japan, *Hiroshima University Management Studies*, **16**, 17–29 (in Japanese).

Hwang, J. and Hopkins, K. (2012). Organizational Inclusion, Commitment, and Turnover among Child Welfare Workers: A Multilevel Mediation Analysis, *Administration in Social Work*, **36**(1), 23–39.

Kim, H. J., Shin, K. H., and Swanger, N. (2009). Burnout and Engagement: A Comparative Analysis Using the Big Five Personality Dimensions, *International Journal of Hospitality Management*, **28**(1), 96–104.

Kline, R. B. (2015). *Principles and Practice of Structural Equation Modeling*, 4th ed., Guildford Press, New York.

Komatsu, M. (2007). The Beginning of the Journey, in Toyoda, H., ed., *Covariance Structural Analysis [Amos ed.]: Structural Equation Modeling*, Tokyo Tosho (in Japanese), Tokyo.

Laczo, R. M. and Hanisch, K. A. (1999). An Examination of Behavioral Families of Organizational Withdrawal in Volunteer Workers and Paid Employees, *Human Resource Management Review*, **9**(4), 453–477.

Magoshi, E. and Chang, E. (2009). Diversity Management and the Effects on Employees' Organizational Commitment: Evidence from Japan and Korea, *Journal of World Business*, **44**(1), 31–40.

Mor Barak, M. E., Lizano, E. L., Kim, A., Duan, L., Rhee, M. K., Hsiao, H. Y., and Brimhall, K. C. (2016). The Promise of Diversity Management for Climate of Inclusion: A State-of-the-Art Review and Meta-analysis, *Human Service Organizations: Management, Leadership and Governance*, **40**(4), 305–333.

Nakamura, Y. (2017). Diversity and Inclusion: Basic Concept, Historical Transition and Significance, *Takachiho Review*, **52**(1), 53–84 (in Japanese).

Nakamura, Y. (2018). Diversity and Inclusion in Japanese Firms: Current Status and Issues, *Takachiho Review*, **53**(2), 21–99 (in Japanese).

Nishii, L. H. (2013). The Benefits of Climate for Inclusion for Gender-Diverse Groups, *Academy of Management Journal*, **56**(6), 1754–1774.

Okada, K. and Yoshida, Y. (2019). Five Essentials of Engagement Management for Japanese Companies to Win the War for Talent (Special Feature: Employee Engagement), *Harvard Business Review*, **44**(11), 76–90 (in Japanese).

Okubo, S. (2014). *Companies Where Women Are Active*, Nihon Keizai Shimbun Publishing Inc, Tokyo (in Japanese).

Saks, A. M. (2006). Antecedents and Consequences of Employee Engagement, *Journal of Managerial Psychology*, **21**(7), 600–619.

Schaufeli, W. B. and Bakker, A. B. (2004). Job Demands, Job Resources, and Their Relationship with Burnout and Engagement: A Multi-sample Study, *Journal of Organizational Behavior*, **25**(3), 293–315.

Schaufeli, W. B., Salanova, M., González-Romá, V., and Bakker, A. B. (2002). The Measurement of Engagement and Burnout: A Two Sample Confirmatory Factor Analytic Approach, *Journal of Happiness Studies*, **3**(1), 71–92.

Suzuki, R. (2013). *Management of Engaged Workplaces*, Yuhikaku, Tokyo (in Japanese).

Thomas, R. R. (1991). *Beyond Race and Gender*, AMACOM, New York.

Thoresen, C. J., Kaplan, S. A., Barsky, A. P., Warren, C. R., and de Chermont, K. (2003). The Affective Underpinnings of Job Perceptions and Attitudes: A Meta-analytic Review and Integration, *Psychological Bulletin*, **129**(6), 914–945.

Waki, Y. (2019). A Study of Conceptual Differences between Diversity and Inclusion, *Journal of Business and Economics*, **60**(2) (in Japanese), 33–44.

Part 3

Network Management for Symbiosis

Chapter 10

Management Accounting for Digital Twin-Driven New Product Development in a Sustainable Supply Chain

Yoshiteru Minagawa

Nagoya Gakuin University, Nagoya, Japan

1. Introduction

The main role of sustainable supply chain management is to strengthen cooperation among customers and partners to enhance the three elements of sustainable competitiveness and development — economic, social, and environmental value — for customers and stakeholders in a harmonized and integrated manner (Seuring and Muller, 2008). This raises an important question: How is value created? One potential answer is that satisfaction brings about value (Woodside *et al.*, 2008; Macdivitt and Wilkinson, 2012). Therefore, to determine how to create value, we first need to clarify for whom the value is being created (Boruchowitch and Ftitz, 2022). For a firm, economic value is derived from customer satisfaction with products and services it offers, which is the fundamental factor of corporate social responsibility. Social value emerges from satisfaction gained by the key stakeholders involved in the firm. Environmental value concerns the Earth's survival, which is one of the biggest issues for humankind at present. Disclosing increases the economic, social, and environmental value of the firm and allows it to obtain trust and reputation in society, boosting its product or service sales, and subsequently improving its economic value.

In this study, we examine how to build an interfirm trust relationship. One factor positively affecting trust among the partners of a supply chain is willingness to assist in the reduction of other partners' risks (Das and Teng, 1998, p. 504). Furthermore, the development of a trusting relationship among a supply chain requires that all the partners commonly expect others to perform a specific action that will increase their benefit (Mayer *et al.*, 1995, p. 712). One way to create and promote such incentive alignment across the entire supply chain is to form and implement a management control system in which each partner's profit is considerably affected by the overall supply chain profit. Therefore, the achievement of goal congruence is necessary; this is one of the research questions.

This study examines the strategic benefits of three management approaches that can help achieve the supply chain sustainability. One of the key activities that raises the economic value of the supply chain is the management of a network-wide collaborative new product development (NPD) involving customers. There are two critical success factors of partnership-based NPD. The first requirement is to provide information about the target customers' needs that the supply chains should strive to meet, based on collaboration among all partners. The second is to implement NPD projects in which all involved firms have a solid understanding of how well each partner is accomplishing its role in NPD. Another managerial practice that contributes to the social potential of a supply chain is the equitable allocation of economic profit of the supply chain among partner members. A firm is responsible for providing benefits to its stakeholders, such as government, consumers, employees, suppliers, distributors, shareholders, industry peers, social groups, and the public, in a fair manner (Li *et al.*, 2020, p. 13). Thus, a sustainable supply chain should establish a rational allocation of its total profit among members to efficiently integrate all partners' collaborative efforts into the enhanced economic value. Finally, to increase environmental value, it is important to develop new products that can reduce carbon emissions.

The three sustainable growth factors can be mutually integrated using economic value as an analytical base. First, NPD performance success has a great effect on the economic value, which is a contributing factor to the sustainable growth of firms. Sustained NPD success can, in turn, continually generate stable cash flow from business activities, increasing free cash flow available to the firms as sources of investment funds for future projects. One of the key success factors in NPD is to design a product that can achieve target customer satisfaction and be sold at a price commensurate with the customer's perceived value. Moreover, for some customers, satisfaction with a product depends on whether it is carbon-free. How do we develop products that meet target customer value and achieve a target price in the market? This problem will be addressed in this study.

Second, a managerial activity that can help improve social value in a sustainable supply chain is to rationally distribute the supply chain's overall profit among its partners. Given that a supply chain's total profit is a result of the collective efforts of all members, fair allocation of profits among its members is necessary. Transfer pricing in a supply chain can influence the effectiveness of partners' incentives to increase the supply chain's total profit. This study examines the strategic relevance of a supply chain's internal-transfer pricing approach, which uses a customer-perceived value-based price for pricing a transaction between partners.

Based on the aforementioned viewpoint, this study examines NPD methods relevant to improving economic, social, and environmental values to build a sustainable supply chain. To achieve this, technological innovation is essential (Li *et al.*, 2020, p. 13). A company's technology includes product technology related to NPD and design, manufacturing, marketing, and business administration. This study considers the positive impact of a digital twin (DT) on the management control of NPD that generates high profit margins in a sustainable supply chain.

We are currently in the digital age. Therefore, it is important for firms to fully understand how to leverage digital technologies to create new customer values and experiences. DTs are one of the most prevalent digital technologies today (Havard *et al.*, 2019; Jones *et al.*, 2020).

Specifically, a DT can digitally copy and reproduce any real-world entity or system, such as products and production processes, in virtual space throughout their entire life cycle in real time. To enable the entire life cycle management of a component and system, a DT performs a simulation based on the virtual replica of a real-world entity to predict its future functionality and operation (Tao *et al.*, 2019). The DT-driven simulation-generating data are visualized based on Virtual Reality (VR) and Augmented Reality (AR) and then fed back to the real world to be shared among all project participants (Tao *et al.*, 2019). Using AR, people in the real world enjoy interactive experiences across the real and virtual worlds. VR interrupts the real world and allows people to enjoy various experiences in various virtual worlds (Hoyer *et al.*, 2020, pp. 3–5).

Furthermore, data generated by DT simulation are fed back to the concerned physical object and used to optimize that object (Lin *et al.*, 2021, p. 2). DTs enable seamless and efficient two-way communication (Wang *et al.*, 2021, p. 272; Jones *et al.*, 2020). Thus, the DT creates a virtual high-fidelity representation of the real world in real time, performs simulations linked to the real world, and feeds back the results to the physical space. Such DT-driven dynamic and real-time simulations enable the entire life cycle asset management.

Winning the competition between supply chains requires development and supply of products or services that can deliver high customer value in the market. One way to successfully overcome this strategic challenge is customer involvement in the early stage of NPD. Customer participation in NPD can be considerably enhanced by leveraging VR and AR because such digital technologies allow consumers to easily access usable visualized information about the products and services using their personal PCs and smartphones, enhancing a connection between consumers and firms (Wang *et al.*, 2021, 2022).

This study examines the excellent managerial practices of NPD in a sustained supply chain from the following analytical perspective. First, a supply chain must effectively and efficiently achieve NPD processes to foster sustainable growth. A relevant performance indicator for identifying NPD best practices is breakeven time (BET) developed by the Hewlett-Packard Company (House and Price, 1991). BET refers to the time lapse between the start of an NPD investment project and breakeven point (House and Price, 1991). There are two main advantages to shortening BET. First, a shorter payback period is associated with less risk compared to a project with a large one. Second, a short BET indicates a greater potential for extending the total period to earn anticipated profits. How can the BET be improved? This study highlights the beneficial impact of DTs on building a collaborative NPD, which results in a shortened BET.

A DT can connect a virtual space with a real space in dynamic and real-time manner. Therefore, a DT-based supply chain enables construction of a high-fidelity DT (Tao *et al.*, 2019). Furthermore, the data from the DT-based simulation are visualized and fed back to the project participants in the real world. Such visual information sharing among partners greatly improves the speed and integration of NPD in the supply chain. The improvement has led to an enhanced BET surface area.

2. DTs' Capability to Enhance Corporate Competitive Advantage

DT concept model is based on the following three factors: real-world items and procedures, digital artifacts in virtual space, and data for connecting real spaces with virtual ones (Grieves, 2014, p. 1). DTs can establish a seamless two-way communication between the real and virtual worlds by transmitting the data collected in a real space to a virtual domain. Moreover, a DT can build a high-fidelity virtual replica of real-world objects based on real-time data in an actual space (Tao *et al.*, 2018, p. 3566; Tao *et al.*, 2019, pp. 3939–3941). Thus, a DT reflects products and production systems in the real world by replicating virtual environments in real time. To achieve this, the DT receives non-stop real-time data about the physical product in the real world. Based on this, it performs dynamic simulations to analyze the virtual replicas (DTs) of real-world physical assets in the virtual space (Tao *et al.*, 2019, p. 7). Thus, a DT can act as a real-time representation of the real world in a virtual space and generate dynamic simulations of real-world objects in a virtual space based on the real-time data of real physical objects. Furthermore, a DT feeds back simulation-generated data to the physical space (Tao *et al.*, 2019, p. 3941; Lin *et al.*, 2021, p. 2).

A DT-based system can create a simulation based on the virtual replicas of a real-world product for data analysis and to predict the future of the product, diagnose issues, and train it. More importantly, a DT can provide feedback from simulations of real-world products to achieve product optimization (Lin *et al.*, 2021, p. 2). DTs collect and generate data in real and virtual spaces (Wang *et al.*, 2021, p. 272). Data gathered from the real world include information/knowledge and data collected by the sensors (Tao *et al.*, 2019, p. 3939). DTs can implement the real-time reflection of real-world data into virtual space. Data collected and generated in the virtual space include simulation-generating data and computer-based analysis-driven information (Wang *et al.*, 2021, p. 272). A DT-based system can visualize information created in a virtual space based on VR technology, enabling information sharing among the participants.

Tao *et al.* (2019, pp. 3940–3941) established the following steps for building a DT:

Step 1: Reproduce a real-world physical product in virtual space based on three-dimensional computer-aided design (3D CAD), that is, build a DT.

Step 2: Integrate multiple data into information by analyzing data obtained from physical products and the Internet of Things (IoT) to enhance decision-making. Visualize the data and information.

Step 3: Digitize the physical product-related data collected in the physical space and simulate it in virtual space. Multiple decision-makers directly participate in the simulation using personal VR.

Step 4: Send the simulation results back into the real world to modify the function, movement, and structure of the physical product.

Step 5: Conduct seamless, real-time, secure, and bidirectional data transmission between the physical product and DT.

3. How to Improve BET

BET is a relevant performance measurement for the management control of NPD. There are two organizational capabilities to improve BET. First, from the outset, when first supplying a new product to the market, it is necessary to sell the product at a price commensurate with the target customers' perceived value of the product. Second, faster time to market is necessary. Strategic effects of fast marketing include gaining exclusive profit in the concerned target segment until others enter the market and extend the product life cycle duration. These two managerial capabilities allow for the early development of new products that can satisfy target customers' needs and deliver them to the customers at a price equivalent to their perceived value.

This study proposes an NPD method based on target pricing and value-based pricing (VBP), which are useful for offering products that can satisfy target customers' needs at customers' perceived value-based selling price. According to Makido (2000, p. 169), "target pricing is the set of activities that first, determine a target price by adding the expected or target cost to the required profit, and then develop and design a new product that can achieve an appropriate customer-perceived value necessary to realize this price in the market." The procedure and features of the NPD method are as follows:

(1) Determine target profit for a new product to be developed based on the company-wide profit plan. One type of profit target for new products is the gross profit margin for goods on sales (Makido, 1985, p. 30), calculated by dividing the difference between net sales and cost of goods sold by net sales.

(2) Determine the customer value that will be achieved by products and services. According to existing research (Woodside *et al.*, 2008; Macdivitt and Wilkinson, 2012), a customer's perceived value for products and services arises after satisfying customer needs. This leads to the following three types of drivers of customers' value:

First, customers seek product features and service effects that are useful in solving the problems faced by them (Woodside *et al.*, 2008, p. 11). The driving factors of customer satisfaction include the product's functions and effectiveness of the service itself. For example, the key features that influence the purchasing decision of an electric vehicle are the maximum driving range on a 100% charge, time required to achieve 100% charge, amount of electricity consumption required for a given driving range, acceleration performance (the time it takes to reach 100 km/h from engine start), and carbon dioxide emissions (Hidrue *et al.*, 2011). Low carbon dioxide emission is the most important differentiating attribute of a gasoline-free car.

(i) Nowadays, societal demand for low-carbon footprints is growing. Thus, many modern product segments face the challenge of developing and supplying low-carbon emission goods. This increases the importance of calculating how much customers are willing to pay to reduce carbon emissions. In the following, we discuss how to calculate the economic benefits of reducing carbon dioxide emissions.

The economic benefits of reducing carbon dioxide emissions can be calculated by multiplying the amount of carbon dioxide reduction (tons) by the carbon price per ton. Carbon pricing is divided into the following two main approaches: the damage cost and abatement cost approaches (Sundqvist, 2004, p. 1755; Kawashima, 2015, p. 4). The former is a monetary assessment of the extent of social damage caused by carbon dioxide (CO_2) emissions (Sundqvist, 2004, p. 1755; Kawashima, 2015, p. 4). This is the social cost of CO_2 emissions. Using this method, the economic benefits of CO_2 emission reductions were determined based on the social costs attributed to them. The latter is based on the costs of mitigating and preventing the social and economic losses caused by CO_2 emissions (Sundqvist, 2004, p. 1755; Kawashima, 2015, p. 4). Therefore, this method assumes that the economic benefits of curbing CO_2 emissions are equal to the cost of emission reduction.

Additionally, the calculation of customer-perceived economic value of carbon emission reduction can also be based on the extent to which customers are willing to pay for this benefit (Small and Kazimi, 1995, p. 14).

(ii) Second is the consumers' desire to effectively and efficiently use the products and services purchased by them (Woodside *et al.*, 2008, p. 11). In other words, consumers want to greatly benefit from solutions provided by the goods. Customer satisfaction can be gauged from a myriad of factors, including safety, economic consideration (efficiency), ease of use (saving time and money), connectivity level, access to information about the product/service, after-sales service quality, and duration between ordering and delivery (Almquist *et al.*, 2016, p. 51).

(iii) Third, consumers pursue psychological satisfaction (Woodside *et al.*, 2008, p. 11), such as security, comfort, peace of mind, assurance, quality, and design.

(3) Identify the reference products or services in the targeted new product field.

(4) Perform a tear-down analysis of the reference products or services to decide the target-price amount of a new product or service needed to realize its target gross profit margin for goods on sales decided in Step 1.

   (i) This analysis focuses on the following three factors of reference goods: the content and grade level of features offered to consumers, selling prices as the monetary equivalent of the customer's perceived value for the goods, and gross profit margin for goods on sales. These data are relevant to the following series of decisions about NPD: What content and grade level of functionality or effectiveness is required to develop the new product or new service? How much should the new product or service be priced to achieve the target gross profit margin for goods on sales in the market?

   The aforementioned analysis assumes that high prices only lead to high gross profit margin for goods on sales if consumers are willing to pay. The justification is that an increase in customers' perceived value of a product's functionality or service effectiveness enhances their purchase intention. This raises the degree to which the increased price exceeds the cost of developing and producing the product or service. Furthermore, this study assumes that the increased price of a new product or service exceeds the increased cost per product.

(5) To achieve the target price of a new product or service in a given market, it is necessary to decide the content and grade level of functionality or effectiveness of the new product or service.

   In the previous procedures, the target price of a new product or service to be developed was decided. Here, the content and grade level of the functionality or effectiveness of the new product or service needed to realize the target prices in the market are decided. The price/value design requires determining the content of and grade level of the product functionality or service effectiveness, which induce the consumers to pay the target prices. Therefore, it is necessary to calculate a customer's perceived value for goods in monetary terms.

(6)   A useful method to calculate customers' perceived value in monetary terms is to apply VBP. The two main managerial practices of VBP include reference price and differentiated value. Smith and Nagle (1995) established that a consumer's decision to purchase a certain product or service is considerably influenced by the amount of monetary gain or loss relative to its reference product for that product or service. This is based on prospect theory (Kahneman and Tversky, 1979). Wouters and Kirchberger (2015) insisted that the best approach for calculating a customer's perceived value of a product is to ascertain the amount of monetary gain or loss relative to its reference product. Such an analytical framework for consumer purchasing psychology achieves the following VBP calculation:

A VBP for a product is its competitive reference product's price + the monetary amount of a product's differentiation value realized by the product's differentiated attributes delivered to the customer over those provided by the reference product (Macdivitt and Wilkinson, 2012, p. 114; Nagale and Müller, 2018, p. 29). Here, a product differentiation value is derived from an attractive attribute that can differentiate the product from its competitors.

How is the differentiation value of a product or service calculated in monetary terms? This requires the following three approaches. The first is the net amount by which the revenues obtained from a product or service exceed those derived from comparable ones (Hinterhuber, 2004; Macdivitt and Wilkinson, 2012, pp. 117–129; Nagale and Müller, 2018, pp. 27–43).

The second are the savings generated using the product or service in question, compared with the savings from the reference product (Macdivitt and Wilkinson, 2012, pp. 117–129; Nagale and Müller, 2018, pp. 27–43). The third concerns the monetary evaluation of customers' psychological satisfaction. This study focuses on using customers' willingness to pay (WTP) as a proxy for their psychological satisfaction. Accordingly, the monetary amount of psychological factor-based customer satisfaction can be estimated by calculating how much customers are willing to pay for such satisfaction (Lau *et al.*, 2013).

(7) Implement design to value/price (DTVP) to design a product that can realize customers' perceived value-based target price in the target product market.

DTVP is a series of engineering and managerial management practices that can create, at a low cost, the product function or service effect necessary to realize customers' value-based target price for the new product or service in the market (Fuchs and Golenhofen, 2019, p. 107). DTVP includes the following two stages: design-to-function (design for the purpose of building into the product, the functionality required to achieve customers' value-driven target price in the market) and design-to-cost (design to achieve the target cost) (Fuchs and Golenhofen, 2019).

DTVP requires data on how much customers are willing to pay in return for the benefits derived from a given product function (Figure 1). Based on this, design-to-function is calculated. In planning a new product, it is essential to have information on the relationship between the product function and cost, that is, the relationship between the cost of a particular product function and the cost of building it into the product. The analytical method, presented by Chilukuri *et al.* (2019) (accessed on March 1, 2023), explains that the information on the impact of product function on cost is used in terms of design-to-cost.

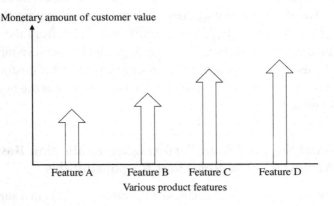

Figure 1. Essential Data for DTVP

Source: Inspired by Chilukuri *et al.* (2019, exhibit 1).

As mentioned in the previous paragraph, a critical decision to achieve the target profit of a new product involves the determination of the products' contents and customers' value of the goods to be developed. This should be based on the price and gross profit on sales of the reference goods. The calculation of how much a customer is willing to pay to fulfill his/her needs using a product can be based on VBP.

4. 3D-CAD

A starting-point technology for DT is the three-dimensional computer-aided design (3D-CAD). Aoshima (1998) empirically and theoretically examined the strategic benefits of Boeing's newly introduced 3D-CAD-based NPD in the B777 development project. Furthermore, their comparative analysis of the Japanese-mode NPD with 3D-CAD-driven NPD clarified the usefulness of integrating the two technologies (Aoshima, 1998).

Aoshima (1998) showed that the essential steps of the B777 development processes include the integration of digitalized design data for components into the 3D-CAD system, which aims to allow all project participants to fulfill their own responsibilities while utilizing all project data.

According to Aoshima (1998), digital transformation in NPD processes can achieve reduction-driven design time flexibility. However, this raises the problem of when to fix the design, that is, when the design should be finalized (Aoshima, 1998, p. 721). In this study, this problem is resolved based on the management policy of not changing the original product plan. Accordingly, the target NPD is decided from the viewpoint of the functions to be included in the new product to achieve target profit. If this method is employed, it is essential to fix the customer value required to achieve the target profit of the new product at the beginning of the NPD project.

5. Internal Supply Chain Performance Evaluation Based on Achievement of Roles and Responsibilities

One of the most important management control practices in a supply chain is aligning partners' incentives to establish sustainable competitive advantages (Narayanan and Raman, 2004). A specific approach to aligning incentives throughout a supply chain is to achieve goal congruence. Goal congruence in a supply chain refers to the extent to which each partner's goal is affected by the achievement of supply chain goals as a whole (Cao *et al.*, 2010). For a supply chain to attain goal congruence, it is essential to clearly determine each partner's responsibility in terms of bringing goods that can meet customers' needs in the markets.

In this study, we examine how to effectively implement goal congruence:

(1) Decide the roles and responsibilities assumed by each member to enhance profitability of the supply chain as a whole.
(2) Develop an information-sharing system, which is essential for accomplishing goal congruence in the partnership.
(3) Establish a relevant management control system to increase the partners' efforts toward achieving their assigned responsibilities. The following is a detailed discussion.

5.1 *Supply chain partners' roles and responsibilities*

This study's theoretical framework on supply chain partnerships in collaborative NPD is as follows: BET is a critical performance indicator for NPD that can sensitively measure effectiveness and efficiency of the ongoing NPD. The improvement measures of BET include developing a product or service that can achieve target customer satisfaction and selling at a target price set up based on customers' perceived value.

Here, we show the steps in the process of determining the target price.

(1) Determine the target gross profit margin for goods on sales that the new product or service should earn to achieve the company-wide profit plan.
(2) Analyze the reference products of an NPD to develop customer-perceived values, prices, and gross profit margins for goods on sales. Further, identify the targeted segment of the customer-perceived value before planning a new product or service.

(3) Determine the features to be added to the new products or services to bring differentiated benefits to the customers. These features may convince them to pay the target selling price. To design a product or service that realizes the target price in the market, it is necessary to convert customers' perceived value of the product functions or effectiveness of service into a monetary value.

Thus, the supply chain objectives and role of partners can be summarized as follows: the objective of the entire supply chain is to attain the target amount of customers' perceived value for the differentiated attributes of a new product. Each part of the supply chain is responsible for quickly designing and producing a component or service that can meet the required attributes and customers' perceived value.

5.2 *Information sharing based on DT*

This section clarifies the extent to which a DT in a supply chain improves the design of a product that meets customers' needs and WTP, achieving targeted profit benefits for the new product.

As stated in the previous section, a DT in a supply chain can realize transparency throughout the entire network as it enables participants to share visualized information about the new product prototype. Here, we clarify that DT-based smart-connected systems can share valuable information in a collaborative NPD project among partners.

(1) A DT can perform a computer simulation using real-time data of the new product prototype received from real space. The simulation results, which are used to predict the future of the new product, are digitalized and fed back to the participants (Tao *et al.*, 2019).

(2) Given that each partner's current work status is reflected in the DT, everyone can understand the work of other partners, using the DT as a lens. Thus, each supply chain member can share the impact of all members' development work on the prototype. Therefore, the DT enables effective and efficient virtual verification of the product development work status of each participant (Tao *et al.*, 2019, p. 3947). This information sharing positively contributes to the effective and efficient implementation of joint development.

(3) The DT-based supply chain's NPD method proposed in this study incorporates customers' perceived value-based transfer price into transactions among supply chain partners. One of the reasons each member in the supply chain fails to fulfill his/her role is insufficient information sharing about other members' management activities (Lee *et al.*, 1997). When there is a lack of communication, we must rely on guesswork. However, guessing is fraught with failure.

The DT-based system in a supply chain's NPD eliminates the issue of inadequate information sharing among partners. Given that it can enable transparency in a collaborative NPD process, all partners can access valuable information, such as the future of the new product, as the results of DT-based dynamic simulations. They can also access each partner's current work status. Such information transparency throughout the supply chain can be instrumental in integrating all partners into a successful collaborative NPD.

To fully ensure the success of developing and supplying products that can highly satisfy target customer needs in a DT-based supply chain, it is necessary to establish and implement management control practices that encourage partners to develop and fabricate product components that can properly meet target customers' needs. The method to provide proper incentives for supply chain partners to create products that are highly valued by the consumers is considered in the following.

The NPD practice discussed in this paper has the following two strategic advantages:

(i) Set a target price necessary to achieve the target profit of the new product or service. This price is determined based on the long-term target profit of the supply chain as a whole.
(ii) Design new product features and effective service for which customers are willing to pay the target price.

One of the key management techniques to effectively and efficiently execute NPD is to insert customers' perceived value-based transfer price in a transaction between supply chain's partners.

Under this method, the transfer price is based on the VBP of goods and services traded between partners. We assume that the internal supply chain transaction rate is 100%. Further, it is also assumed that each partner in a supply chain does not trade with non-partners. This assumption allows us to study the impact of goal congruence (i.e., the extent to which economic performance of each partner in a supply chain is affected by the overall profit of the supply chain). Under VBP-based transfer pricing, a partner's profit is the difference between customers' value-based price for goods and services purchased and costs incurred. Accordingly, under this supply chain transfer pricing scheme, each partner's profit depends largely on whether they have been able to create and supply the product or service that can achieve the target customer value. Thus, under this transfer pricing method, profits earned by each partner in the supply chain are heavily affected by partners' capabilities to create components that satisfy target customers.

How can this transfer price be calculated? In this study, this problem is solved by using a DT and having customers make the determination. In the proposed solution, customers are asked to reproduce the finished prototypes on their personal computers using VR and AR technologies. Further, they are asked to estimate how much they would be willing to pay for the parts and services created by each of the partners in the supply chain. Here is the proposed practice:

(a) Create a 3D digital video that allows people to virtually recognize and perceive the effects of a new product or service's features in the real world.
(b) Transmit the digital images to the consumer.
(c) The consumer experiences the product or service using digital technologies, such as AR, VR, and DT.
(d) The consumer determines how much the product feature is worth.

Digital technology and devices can transform the reactions of the users whose five senses are activated by stimuli in the virtual space and can be used for digital data measurement, enabling the creation of a "presence" that makes the user feel as if they are in the real world (Wedel *et al.*, 2020, p. 446). This is key in enriching customers' experiences. Thus, in this regard, it is essential to create a sense of "presence" in the virtual space. Owing to the benefits generated by digital technology, the customers involved in NPD projects can now measure their perceived value of the goods in monetary terms.

6. Conclusion

This study identified management practices that are useful for effective and efficient implementation of DT-based collaborative NPD in a supply chain. Regarding strategic management indicators, this study focused on BET and presented a specific NPD method for its improvement based on VBP and target pricing. Furthermore, the usefulness of transfer pricing with VBP in promoting goal congruence was also discussed.

References

Almquist, E., Senior, J., and Bloch, N. (2016). The Elements of Value, *Harvard Business Review*, September, pp. 47–53.

Aoshima, Y. (1998). The Japanese Style of New Product Development and the Computer-Based Concurrent Engineering: A Comparison with the Boeing 777 Development Process, *Hitotsubashi Review*, **120**(5), 111–134 (in Japanese).

Boruchowitch, F. and Fritz, M. M. C. (2022). Who in the Firm Can Create Sustainable Value and For Whom? A Single Case-Study on Sustainable Procurement and Supply Chain Stakeholders, *Journal of Cleaner Production*, **363**, https://doi.org/10.1016/j.jclepro.2022.132619.

Cao, M., Vonderembse, M. A., Zhang, Q., and Ragu-Nathan, T. S. (2010). Supply Chain Collaboration: Conceptualization and Instrument Development, *International Journal of Production Research*, **48**(22), 6613–6635.

Chilukuri, S., Gordon, M., Musso, C., and Ramaswamy, S. (2019). Design to Value in Medical Devices, https://www.mckinsey.com/~/media/mckinsey/dotcom/client_service/Pharma%20and%20Medical%20Products/PMP%20NEW/PDFs/774172_Design_to_value_in_medical_devices1.ashx, Viewed on March 1st, 2023.

Das, T. K. and Teng, B. S. (1998). Between Trust and Control: Developing Confidence in Partner Cooperation in Alliances, *Academy of Management Review*, **23**(3), 491–512.

Fuchs, C. and Golenhofen, F. (2019). *Mastering Disruption and Innovation in Product Management: Connecting the Dots*, Springer, New York.

Grieves, M. (2014). Digital Twin: Manufacturing Excellence for Virtual Factory Replication, White Paper, Florida Institute of Technology.

Havard, V., Jeanne, B., Lacomblez, M., and Baudry, D. (2019). Digital Twin and Virtual Reality: A Co-simulation Environment for Design and Assessment of Industrial Workstations, *Production & Manufacturing Research*, **7**(10), 472–489.

Hidrue, M., Parsons, G. R., Kempton, W., and Gardner, M. P. (2011). Willingness to Pay for Electric Vehicles and Their Attributes, *Resource and Energy Economics*, **33**(3), 686–705.

Hinterhuber, A. (2004). Towards Value-Based Pricing — An Integrative Framework for Decision Making, *Industrial Marketing Management*, **33**(1), 765–778.

House, C. H. and Price, R. L. (1991). The Return Map: Tracking Product Teams, *Harvard Business Review*, **69**(19), 92–100.

Hoyer, W. D., Kroschke, M., Schmitt, B., Kraume, K., and Shankar, V. (2020). Transforming the Customer Experience through New Technologies, *Journal of Interactive Marketing*, **51**(4), 51–71.

Jones, D., Snider, C., Nassehi, A., Yon, J., and Hicks, B. (2020). Characterizing the Digital Twin: A Systematic Literature Review, *CIRP Journal of Manufacturing Science and Technology*, **29**, 36–52.

Kahneman, D. and Tversky, A. (1979). Prospect Theory: An Analysis of Decision under Risk, *Econometrica*, **47**(2), 263–291.

Kawashima, Y. (2015). The Assessment of Global Warming, *PRI Review*, **57**, 2–7.

Lau, H. B. P., White, M. P., and Schnall, S. (2013). Quantifying the Value Using a Willingness to Pay Approach, *Journal of Happiness Studies*, **14**, 1543–1561.

Lee, H. L., Padmanabhan, V., and Whang, S. (1997). The Bullwhip Effect in Supply Chains, *Sloan Management Review*, **38**(3), 93–102.

Li, X., Cao, J., Liu, Z., and Luo, X. (2020). Sustainable Business Model Based on Digital Twin Platform Network: The Inspiration from Haier's Case Study in China, *Sustainability*, **12**(3), 1–27.

Lin, T. Y., Shi, G., Yang, C., Zhang, Y., Wang, J., Jia, Z., Guo, L., Xiao, Y., Wei, Z., and Lan, S. (2021). Efficient Container Virtualization-Based Digital Twin Simulation of Smart Industrial Systems, *Journal of Cleaner Production*, **281**, 1–19.

Macdivitt, H. and Wilkinson, M. (2012). *Value-Based Pricing: Drive Sales and Boost Your Bottom Line by Creating, Communicating, and Capturing Customer Value*, The McGraw-Hill Companies, New York.

Makido, T. (1985). Cost Management, in Ogawa, E., ed., *Production Management*, Chuokeizai-sha, Tokyo, pp. 125–147 (in Japanese).

Makido, T. (2000). Characteristics of Japanese Management Accounting and Its Overseas Transfer, *Accounting*, **157**(3), 161–174 (in Japanese).

Mayer, R. C., Davis, J. H., and Schoorman, F. D. (1995). An Integrative Model of Organizational Trust, *Academy of Management Review*, **20**(3), 708–734.

Nagale, T. T. and Müller, G. (2018). *The Strategy and Tactics of Pricing*, Routledge, London.

Narayanan, V. G. and Raman, A. (2004). Aligning Incentives in Supply Chains, *Harvard Business Review*, **81**(11), 94–103.

Seuring, S. and Muller, M. (2008). From a Literature Review to a Conceptual Framework for Sustainable Supply Chain Management, *Journal of Cleaner Production*, **16**(15), 1699–1710.

Small, K. A. and Kazimi, C. (1995). On the Costs of Air Pollution from Motor Vehicles, *Journal of Transport Economics & Policy*, **29**(1), 7–32.

Smith, G. E. and Nagle, T. T. (1995). Frame of Reference and Buyers' Perception of Price and Value, *California Management Review*, **38**(1), 98–116.

Sundqvist, T. (2004). What Causes the Disparity of Electricity Externality Estimates? *Energy Policy*, **32**(15), 1753–1766.

Tao, F., Cheng, J., Qi, Q., Zhang, M., Zhang, H., and Sui, F. (2018). Digital Twin-Driven Product Design, Manufacturing and Service with Big Data, *International Journal of Advanced Manufacturing Technology*, **94**(4), 3563–3576.

Tao, F., Sui, A. L., Qi, Q., Zhang, M., Song, B., Guo, Z., Lu, S. C. Y., and Nee, A. Y. C. (2019). Digital Twin-Driven Product Design Framework, *International Journal of Production Research*, **57**(1), 3935–3953.

Wang, X., Wang, Y., Tao, F., and Liu, A. (2021). New Paradigm of Data-Driven Smart Customisation through Digital Twin, *Journal of Manufacturing Systems*, **58**, 270–280.

Wang, L., Deng, T., Shen, Z. M., Hu, H., and Qi, Y. (2022). Digital Twin-Driven Smart Supply Chain, *Frontiers of Engineering Management*, **9**(1), 56–70.

Wedel, M., Bigne, E., and Zhang, J. (2020). Virtual and Augmented Reality: Advancing Research in Consumer Marketing, *International Journal of Research in Marketing*, **37**(3), 443–465.

Woodside, A. G., Golfetto, F., and Gibbert, M. (2008). Customer Value: Theory, Research, and Practice, in Woodside, A. G., Golfetto, F., and Gibbert, M., eds., *Creating and Managing Superior Customer Value*, JAI Press, Copenhagen, pp. 3–25.

Wouters, M. and Kirchberger, M. A. (2015). Customer Value Propositions as Interorganizational Management Accounting to Support Customer Collaboration, *Industry Marketing Management*, **46**, 54–67.

Chapter 11

The Effects of Compliance on Sustainable Management in Japanese Waterworks Utilities

Kozo Suzuki

Bureau of Waterworks, Tokyo Metropolitan Government
Tokyo, Japan

1. Introduction: Sustainability and Compliance

This study discusses the necessity of compliance efforts to ensure the sustainability of Japanese waterworks utilities and their potential to become a new management approach.

Many Japanese waterworks utilities and their facilities and pipelines built in large numbers during the era of rapid economic growth are aging with the risk of major earthquakes and need to be renewed. Moreover, the population decline is expected to reduce water supply revenues. In such an environment, the trust and understanding of various stakeholders, including customers (rate-paying consumers = residents) and the government, are crucial for large-scale investments to sustain operations.

However, in recent years, the Tokyo Metropolitan Government's Bureau of Waterworks has been plagued by a series of scandals that have undermined its credibility as a waterworks utility. Therefore, the bureau is doing everything in its power to ensure compliance. These efforts are beginning to take precedence over traditional business management methods, such as budgets, personnel, and various plans, which have brought a new management approach to waterworks utilities.

This study evaluates the relationship between corporate scandals and compliance to show that ensuring the sustainability of Japanese waterworks utilities is founded on compliance. An overview of misconduct and compliance programs in the Tokyo Metropolitan Government's Waterworks Bureau is also presented. Then, based on the perspectives of previous studies, we examine the prospects for compliance in waterworks utilities.

According to the Ministry of Health, Labour and Welfare (2019), "Water supply is the totality of facilities that supply water as water fit for human consumption by means of pipelines and other structures." "In principle, waterworks utility shall be managed by the local government." A waterworks utility is defined as "a business that supplies water to meet general demand by means of a water supply" and "since about 1965, mainly during the period of high economic growth, they have been developed and spread throughout the country (97.9% penetration rate in FY2008)." The number of waterworks utilities "still exceeds 6,000 nationwide," of which 1,355 are waterworks utilities and 5,133 are small-scale waterworks.

Japanese waterworks utilities are among the best in the world. Across the country, the water quality is so good that one can drink tap water directly from the faucet. Not only that, but the Tokyo Metropolitan Government's waterworks utility maintains a leakage rate of about 3% due to ongoing leakage prevention measures. It has one of the lowest leakage rates in the world (Tokyo Metropolitan Government Bureau of Waterworks, 2020a, pp. 1–6).

2. Overview of the Literature

Aoki's (2021, pp. 18–30) seminal study on the relationship between scandals and compliance in the private sector in Japan analyzes listed companies (non-financial business corporations ($N = 13,867$) from fiscal years 2009–2013) (Aoki, 2021, pp. 18–30).

This study divides corporate scandals into intentional scandals (accounting fraud, forgery or falsification, and legal violations) and accidental scandals (product failures, operational failures, and moral hazards). Legal violations include collusion, cartels, and improper payments; operational failures include information leaks, construction accidents, and hazardous material leaks; and moral hazard includes embezzlement of funds and other personal crimes, harassment in the workplace, and unethical behavior.

The report states that corporate governance has a restraining effect on corporate scandals, such as "outside directors from the parent company and outside directors who concurrently manage other companies' work toward curbing scandals." On the other hand, it states that "effective governance differs depending on the type of the scandal" and "there are some scandals that cannot be prevented by governance" (Aoki, 2021).

Kato and Ito (2021, pp. 143–145) discuss the relationship between human psychology and organizational management regarding quality scandals that had become the norm at a company. It includes a perspective on continuous scandals. Their study states, "It is necessary to develop people who are able to take a firm stand against wrongdoing, even if they are instructed to do so, and to foster the organizational structure (which is not simply a matter of governance) and organizational culture that will enable them to take the right action."

Aizawa (2018, pp. 13–18) notes the importance of compliance activities to keep the incident from fading away.

There are many examples of anti-corruption and compliance measures in national and local governments. However, we have found neither any analysis of consecutive cases in the limited field of water utilities operated by local governments nor any quantitative verification of the effectiveness of measures to prevent misconduct.

The Tokyo Metropolitan Government's Bureau of Waterworks uncovered three scandals in six years and immediately began to develop programs to ensure compliance including the prevention of corruption.

In 2019, the Tokyo Waterworks Group Compliance Expert Committee consisting of outside experts was newly established. As a result, a system was established to provide supervision, guidance, and advice on compliance for the entire Tokyo Waterworks Group including the Bureau of Waterworks, Tokyo Metropolitan Government (Tokyo Waterworks Group Compliance Expert Committee, 2019, pp. 1–2).

However, the verification of this program is a problem to be solved in the future. This is because it is not only early days since the establishment of the program but it is also uncertain whether statistical processing is possible.

The Tokyo Metropolitan Government (the Bureau of Waterworks is one of the departments of the Tokyo Metropolitan Government) established the "Basic Compliance Policy in Tokyo" in May 2017 (Tokyo Metropolitan Government, 2017, p. 1), which defines the compliance details that employees should recognize. The first of these is "compliance with laws and regulations, as well as with various rules and policies established and decided by the Tokyo Metropolitan Government for the execution of operations." The second is "to constantly reexamine the duties in charge from the perspective of whether they are fulfilling the mission of the Metropolitan Government as expected by the citizens of Tokyo, and to realize a better metropolitan government."

Considering this, compliance in the context of this study is "the observance of laws, regulations, and official rules and policies established for the conduct of business, and the constant striving to achieve the required mission."

Additionally, the behaviors to be eliminated or prevented by this compliance program include intentional misconduct and harassment (belonging to the moral hazard category of accidental misconduct) as classified by Aoki (2021, pp. 18–30). However, water utility employees have a special situation, as they are local public servants. Therefore, bribery and abuse of authority are considered violations of the law, which are classified as intentional misconduct. Simultaneously, information leaks, which are classified as accidental misconduct, are also intentional misconduct if caused intentionally.

3. Sustainability Problems in Japanese Waterworks Utilities

Water resources are essential not only for human survival but also for supporting urban activities and industries. In 2015, the United Nations General Assembly adopted sustainable development goals (SDGs), which defined "water" as one of the goals to achieve a sustainable world. Hence, the sustainability of the entity supplying the water supply is also important.

However, Japanese waterworks utilities today face a variety of problems in ensuring the sustainability of their operations (Tokyo Metropolitan Government Bureau of Waterworks, 2020b, pp. 12–13).

First, facilities developed during the period of rapid economic growth from the late 1950s to the 1970s are aging, and there are approximately 20,000 cases of water leakage and facility damage (accidents) each year. The percentage of water pipelines that have exceeded their useful life is also increasing every year, and it will take more than 130 years to renew all pipelines. The percentage of all water pipeline extensions in Japan (676,500 km) that exceeded their legal service life (40 years) was 14.8% in FY2016 (Ministry of Health, Labour and Welfare, 2019, p. 6). The current annual renewal of the system is 5,057 km, with a renewal rate of 0.75% (FY2016). The number of pipelines that need to be renewed in the next 20 years is projected to be 153,700 km, which is approximately 23% of the total that was constructed before 1980. Moreover, the risk of prolonged water outages due to a major earthquake is increasing because water pipelines have not yet been made earthquake-resistant.

Second, management may continue to face difficulties in the future, as revenues are expected to decrease due to the declining population. In about 30% of the water utilities, the cost of water supply exceeds the unit cost of supply, which may lead to a sharp increase in water rates.

In the case of the Tokyo Metropolitan Government, the scale of the project is large, which enlarges the problems (Tables 1 and 2). Currently, facilities (dams and other raw water facilities, water treatment plants, water distribution reservoirs, and pump stations) and pipelines (water transmission and distribution pipelines) that were intensively and massively constructed during the period of rapid economic growth face a period of renewal. Certain important facilities have remained in use for more than 60 years since their completion. Renewing them involves financial difficulties as well as the difficulty of completely deactivating facilities that are still in use.

In preparation for major earthquakes, since the 1960s, the Tokyo Metropolitan Government's Bureau of Waterworks has been replacing

Table 1. Waterworks Utilities in Major Cities (Japan)

	Tokyo	Sapporo	Yokohama	Nagoya	Osaka
Population served (person)	13,615,467	1,965,008	3,762,046	2,457,438	2,753,819
Water pipeline extension (km)	28,115	6,136	9,433	8,604	5,220
Number of water supply units (units)	7,821,887	975,702	1,907,706	1,345,832	1,657,581
Number of staff (persons)	3,742	657	1,570	1,335	1,331
Water supply Capacity (m3/day)	6,844,500	835,200	1,820,000	1,424,000	2,430,000
Maximum daily water distribution (m3)	4,531,800	583,760	1,203,800	816,694	1,177,600

Source: Tokyo Metropolitan Government Bureau of Waterworks (2021a, pp. 164–165).

Table 2. Waterworks Utilities in Foreign Cities

	Tokyo	London	New York	Paris
Water supply population (million)	1,362	1,010	900	218
Pipeline extension (km)	28,115	32,186	11,095	2,050
Number of staff (persons)	3,742	6,296	5,910	900
One-day average water Distribution (thousand m^3/day)	4,222	2,600	3,785	512

Source: Tokyo Metropolitan Government Bureau of Waterworks (2021a, p. 165).

cast iron pipes, which are vulnerable to external impact, with ductile iron pipes that have superior viscosity and strength. Currently, the water distribution pipeline renewal work is almost complete. However, old water distribution pipelines are scattered in locations where replacement work is difficult, such as busy intersections and downtown areas. This increases the risk of earthquake damage to those locations.

The imminence of an earthquake directly under the Tokyo metropolitan area has been noted. In this context, it is important to improve the seismic resistance of the joints of water distribution pipes that supply water to important facilities. Planned renewal of pipelines based on their deteriorated condition is also essential.

However, Tokyo Metropolitan Government's population is expected to peak in 2025. By 2042, the population is projected to decline by approximately 16% from its peak. As a result, water supply revenues are also expected to decline in line with the decrease in population by approximately 12% in 2040 compared to 2020 (Tokyo Metropolitan Government Bureau of Waterworks, 2020b, pp. 14–15).

4. The Importance of Compliance in Waterworks Utilities and Its Legal Status in Japan

In Japan, Waterworks Law enacted in 1962 (Showa 37) defines the purpose, management entity, and obligations of waterworks utilities. The purpose is to "contribute to the improvement of public health and the living environment through the provision of clean, abundant, and inexpensive water" (Article 1). Waterworks utilities must be approved by the Ministry of Health, Labour and Welfare (Article 6). In principle, the waterworks utility is managed by the local government, that is, publicly owned (Article 6-2). In FY2024, the jurisdiction of the waterworks utility is scheduled to be transferred from the Ministry of Health, Labour and Welfare to the Ministry of Land, Infrastructure, Transport and Tourism and the Ministry of the Environment.

The reasons for the strong public regulation of waterworks utilities are as follows: waterworks utility is directly connected to the daily lives of the people and is essential for maintaining and promoting their health, water is a precious resource, and the utility is a regional monopoly. Waterworks utilities are obligated to provide clean, abundant, and affordable water to consumers upon their request. In the case of the Bureau of Waterworks of the Tokyo Metropolitan Government, the responsibility to provide a stable supply of safe, delicious, high-quality water as a key lifeline that supports the lives of Tokyo residents and the urban activities of the capital city remains unchanged.

Moreover, as mentioned above, for waterworks utilities that are public enterprises, large facilities, such as water purification plants and distribution reservoirs, and the replacement and renewal of long distribution pipelines require financial resources. These efforts are financed by water supply revenue (sales) from users, but this rate of revenue is expected to decrease due to the declining population.

In addition to a decrease in staff, the manpower required for the construction of large-scale facilities and the replacement and renewal of pipelines may decrease. As a result, increases in labor and construction contracting costs are inevitable.

Therefore, to steadily promote the measures, it is important to understand many stakeholders, including the national and relevant local governments and water users. It may be necessary to raise water rates to finance the replacement and renewal of facilities and pipelines. This can be an increased financial burden for customers. Furthermore, the understanding and cooperation of residents (water supply consumers) are necessary for road closures, traffic congestion, noise, and other problems associated with pipeline reconstruction.

Waterworks utilities have a large absolute number of customers because of their regional monopoly grant, and they have a high diversity of stakeholders. Therefore, the scope of the business is also wide. Moreover, local governments are under the control of elected leaders and local councils. Because residents and consumers have a strong influence over waterworks utilities, as the owners and consumers of the utility, their trust and confidence must be earned continually.

5. Scandals at the Tokyo Metropolitan Government's Bureau of Waterworks

However, in the case of the Tokyo Metropolitan Government's Bureau of Waterworks, scandals occurred three times within a six-year period, which could have undermined the trust of customers, the public, and others.

The first scandal was a bribery case in 2012 (Tokyo Metropolitan Government Bureau of Waterworks, Headquarters for Corruption Prevention, 2012, pp. 1–3). An employee who had been working at the bureau until March of the same year provided information about his duties in connection with the construction of a material storage facility to a business operator and received food and entertainment in return. As a result, the employee was arrested in September of the same year and charged with simple bribery (first sentence of Article 197, paragraph 1 of the Penal Code).

The second case was an information leak in 2014 (Tokyo Metropolitan Government Bureau of Waterworks, Headquarters for Corruption Prevention, 2014, pp. 1–4). Three employees (A, B, and C) who worked at the same bureau office were found to have leaked information on minimum price limits to a former employee (X) who ran a consulting firm and a construction contractor (Y) in connection with competitive bidding for several equipment projects.

The third case was an administrative investigation by the Fair Trade Commission in 2018 (Tokyo Waterworks Group Compliance Expert Committee, 2020, pp. 1–7). In October 2018, the Fair Trade Commission conducted an administrative investigation of the bureau based on suspicion of collusion in the contracting process for the "outsourcing of the operation and management of a wastewater treatment facility at a water purification plant" ordered by the bureau. Therefore, a "Special Investigation Team," set up by the Tokyo Metropolitan Government, investigated the matter. As a result, an employee was found to have leaked the "design unit price" for this contract to the outsourced contractor. On July 11, 2019, the Tokyo Metropolitan Government and the Tokyo Metropolitan Waterworks Bureau received a request for improvement measures from the Fair Trade Commission.

Around the same time, another scandal was uncovered at Tokyo Suido Service Company (TSS). In April 2020, Tokyo Suido Service Co. Ltd., which had been entrusted with water purification and distribution services by the Tokyo Metropolitan Government Bureau of Waterworks, merged with PUC Corporation, which was engaged in the development and operation of the bureau's rate-collecting system and other waterworks utility, to form Tokyo Waterworks (TW). The surviving company is PUC Co. The Tokyo Metropolitan Government Bureau of Waterworks and TW form the "Tokyo Waterworks Group." The company was entrusted by the Tokyo Metropolitan Government's Bureau of Waterworks with important operations supervised by the Tokyo Metropolitan Government. The findings included meetings with contractors involving food and drink, false reports of inspections that had not been performed, and instructions to falsify photos of dredging during construction supervision (Tokyo Metropolitan Government, 2019, p. 1).

6. Strengthening Compliance at the Bureau of Waterworks, Tokyo Metropolitan Government

These scandals have eroded confidence in the Tokyo Metropolitan Government's Bureau of Waterworks and the Tokyo Waterworks Group. The risk went beyond the dimension of legal violations and had a negative impact on the sustainability of the waterworks utility. Therefore, in November 2018, the "Interim Report of the Special Investigation Team" was compiled. This report describes the direct prevention of recurrence and prevention of recurrence that captures the structural aspects of the bureau's business.

In April 2019, the Tokyo Metropolitan Government Water Supply Group Compliance Expert Committee was established. In 2020, it formulated an interim report. In March 2021, a report was formulated on the governance of the Tokyo Waterworks Group, including measures to prevent recurrence and compliance not only by the waterworks bureau but also by the policy partner organizations (Tokyo Suido Co. Ltd.).

In April 2021, the bureau began systematizing and operating an "internal control system" that included compliance initiatives, inspections, and improvements (Tokyo Metropolitan Government Bureau of Waterworks, 2021b, pp. 1–3). This is also related to the results of a study on internal controls in local governments by experts for the Ministry of Internal Affairs and Communications (MIC) from 2007 to 2009 (MIC, 2009, pp. 1–6).

This initiative consists of four stages: In the first stage (development of internal controls), possible risks related to the occurrence of scandals associated with violations of laws and regulations of business operations are analyzed, assessed for materiality, and the risks that should be addressed intensively are selected.

In the second stage (operation of internal controls), risks of scandals occurring in all workplaces are identified, and countermeasures are taken and implemented. Then, in the day-to-day execution of business, measures to prevent scandals as stipulated in the Compliance Program are implemented. Efforts are also made to ensure group governance for the policy partnership organizations under the bureau's jurisdiction.

In the third stage (evaluation of internal control), an evaluation of the performance regarding internal control is conducted for each fiscal year.

The results of the evaluation are prepared as an independent "Internal Control Evaluation Report." In addition, from the perspective of maintaining the stability and public interest of the waterworks utility, external evaluations are also incorporated. The issues identified by the evaluation are reflected in the following year's efforts after considering the opinions of external experts.

In the fourth stage (publication of the "Internal Control Evaluation Report"), the report is published with the opinion of the "Tokyo Waterworks Group Compliance Expert Committee."

All these initiatives are targeted at all workplaces. A "Compliance Promotion Plan" is formulated for each workplace, which is then implemented throughout the waterworks bureau. Risks in each business and workplace are also identified. Then, measures to manage them are confirmed and implemented.

Several compliance training sessions for all staff members will also be provided. To promote compliance, months are set aside (April and November). In each workplace, risks are identified through discussions among staff members and opinions exchanged between managers and general staff members. One of the compliance training programs is for all employees with the Director of the Tokyo Metropolitan Government's Bureau of Waterworks as the instructor. The Department of Waterworks as a whole is evaluated on the results of daily inspections at each workplace. For this, a committee of experts (a third-party organization) is consulted.

Institutionally, local public corporations are not required to have auditors or outside directors; rather, a "Committee of Experts" supplements this.

The above programs create an environment to ensure that operations are performed accurately and fraud is unlikely to occur. This leads to the establishment of a system in which employees can work with peace of mind and pride while efficiently and effectively implementing operations.

These include the following effects: Inappropriate and high-risk cases are counted. Staff's awareness of compliance through workplace discussions is raised, which can be considered small group activities. The program also aims to revitalize communication and exchange of opinions in the workplace. The company is also informing vendors of its whistle-blower system.

However, problems have emerged (Tokyo Metropolitan Government Waterworks Bureau, 2022, p. 7). For example, communication within the workplace needs to be facilitated, which also applies to interorganizational communication. The main risks assumed by compliance efforts are mismanagement of contract information and corruption. However, departments that handle information on demand tend to be more concerned about the leakage of personal information. In addition, a sense of "compliance fatigue" from the uniform and overburdened efforts has become apparent.

7. Directions for Preventing Recurrence of Misconduct at the Bureau of Waterworks, Tokyo Metropolitan Government

It is still too early to verify the effectiveness of these efforts. The question remains whether a statistical analysis is possible. Therefore, we examine the efforts of the Tokyo Metropolitan Government's Bureau of Waterworks based on related studies. In the private sector, it is well established that stronger compliance means stronger governance.

However, Aoki (2021, pp. 18–30) states the following: "With regard to accidental misconduct, (omitted) steady efforts on a daily basis, such as improving business processes, are necessary." Their study concludes the following: "Even for malicious misconduct, such as forgery and falsification, governance reforms have their limits, and ongoing corporate efforts, such as the solid operation of an internal reporting system and the spread of ethics, are required."

Thus, steady, continuous efforts are needed to manage intentional misconduct, which is highly malignant in nature, such as forgery or falsification and violation of laws and regulations, and accidental misconduct, such as information leakage. These efforts can include improving business processes, establishing an effective whistleblowing system, and instilling ethics.

Although the scandals at the bureau appear to correspond to accidental scandals described by Aoki (2021, pp. 18–30), in reality, they are similar to intentional scandals owing to their status as public servants.

Therefore, it is essential that these efforts continue to prevent scandals, such as bribery and information leaks (breach of confidentiality), that have continued to occur at the bureau.

The bureau's compliance programs are repeated, ongoing, and thoroughly implemented on a small-group basis. Risks are identified, workplace discussions are held with the participation of all employees, and training is provided for all employees. These methods fulfill the results of the Aoki (2021, pp. 18–30) analysis.

In addition, Aizawa (2018, pp. 13–18) focuses on a company that "internally developed a code of ethics based on a company-wide questionnaire and also initiated small group activities twice a year as compliance activities to keep the incident from fading away." In this study, the company's "compliance activities became more active internally as well, and a new structure of activities and legitimate programs were established." Steady compliance activities like this have begun to be implemented by the Tokyo Metropolitan Government Waterworks Bureau. Therefore, it can be expected that the compliance activities of the Tokyo Metropolitan Government's Bureau of Waterworks will be effective in the future.

These activities also overlap with what Kato and Ito (2021, pp. 143–145) point out as "fostering organizational structures and organizational cultures that enable people to take the right actions."

From these studies, the following can be derived. It is necessary to ensure that there is substantial compliance within the organization. To do so, fostering a favorable corporate culture and building up a continuous and steady series of initiatives that extend to the activities of each and every employee are important. Those are different dimensions of strengthening corporate governance.

8. Summary and Conclusion

Waterworks utilities have traditionally been managed through a system of budgeting, planning, and personnel. However, these management methods were insufficient to ensure compliance.

Therefore, compliance efforts at the Tokyo Metropolitan Government's Bureau of Waterworks are being developed in a manner that prioritizes conventional management methods. It is not only an aspect of "binding" the actions of each staff member. If staff members are compliant in accordance with the code of conduct, they are not disadvantaged and can perform their duties with peace of mind. Ultimately, it also increases the confidence of consumers and the citizens of Tokyo in the waterworks utility and contributes to its sustainability. Therefore, compliance programs are expected to be effective as a new management approach for waterworks utilities.

Waterworks utilities require large-scale facilities. Large amounts of civil engineering work are also implemented. As a result, the probability of personal injury resulting from facility management and construction work is not low. It can be noted that this is similar to compliance, as safety is the top priority in business operations when human lives are involved.

Therefore, safety management, along with compliance, should be deployed as a top priority, including for general business managers and employees. No people inside or outside the organization can oppose compliance and safety, and it is becoming one of the ways to prevent the abandonment of corporate value, thereby increasing it.

However, it is important to continually pursue the optimal method that is compatible with the company's organizational structure, business type, and history. This enables organized, qualitative, and objective compliance efforts that may lead to the establishment of compliance in a way that goes beyond conventional management methods.

References

Aizawa, A. (2018). A Study on Institutional Inbreeding in Compliance Activities of Japanese Firms, *Proceedings of the Conference of the Organization Studies Association of Japan*, **7**(2), 13–18 (in Japanese).

Aoki, H. (2021). The Impact of Corporate Governance on Corporate Scandals, *Organization Science*, **55**(2), 18–30 (in Japanese).

Kato, Y. and Ito, K. (2021). Is it Possible to Return to a Quality Nation? A Study of Human Psychology and Organizational Management Concerning Quality Scandals, *Abstracts of the 51st Annual Meeting of the Society for Quality Control*, November 13, 2021, pp. 143–145 (in Japanese).

Ministry of Health, Labour and Welfare (2019). *Recent Developments in Water Supply Administration* (in Japanese). https://www.mhlw.go.jp/content/1090 0000/000486455.pdf (viewed May 27, 2022).

Ministry of Internal Affairs and Communications (2009). *Final Report of the Study Group on Internal Control in Local Governments (Summary)* (in Japanese). https://www.soumu.go.jp/main_content/000019096.pdf (viewed May 27, 2022).

Tokyo Metropolitan Government (2017). *Tokyo Metropolitan Government Basic Compliance Policy* (in Japanese). https://www.soumu.metro.tokyo.lg.jp/23 compliance/pdf/kihonhousin.pdf (viewed May 27, 2022).

Tokyo Metropolitan Government (2019). *Results of the Special Supervision of Tokyo Suido Service Corporation (TSS)* (Press Release) (in Japanese). https://www.metro.tokyo.lg.jp/tosei/hodohappyo/press/2019/02/22/10.html (viewed May 27, 2022).

Tokyo Waterworks Group Compliance Expert Committee (2019). *First Meeting of the Tokyo Waterworks Group Compliance Expert Committee in Fiscal Year 2019 (Summary of Proceedings)* (in Japanese). https://www.waterworks.metro.tokyo.lg.jp/files/items/28535/File/giji_1.pdf (viewed May 27, 2022).

Tokyo Metropolitan Government Bureau of Waterworks (2020a). *Environmental Five-Year Plan 2020–2024.* https://www.waterworks.metro.tokyo.lg.jp/files/items/30214/File/environment2020-2024.pdf (viewed May 27, 2022).

Tokyo Metropolitan Government Bureau of Waterworks (2020b). *Toward the Realization of Sustainable Tokyo Waterworks: Tokyo Waterworks Long-Term Strategic Concept 2020* (in Japanese). https://www.waterworks.metro.tokyo.lg.jp/files/items/28582/File/01_zentai.pdf (viewed May 27, 2022).

Tokyo Metropolitan Government Bureau of Waterworks (2021a). *Outline of Operations.* September 2021.

Tokyo Metropolitan Government Bureau of Waterworks (2021b). *Tokyo Metropolitan Government Bureau of Waterworks Policy on Internal Control* (in Japanese). https://www.waterworks.metro.tokyo.lg.jp/files/items/30164/File/01.pdf (viewed May 27, 2022).

Tokyo Metropolitan Government Waterworks Bureau (2022). *FY2021 Third Meeting of Tokyo Waterworks Group Compliance Expert Committee (Minutes)* (in Japanese). https://www.waterworks.metro.tokyo.lg.jp/files/items/35706/File/03.pdf (viewed May 27, 2022).

Tokyo Metropolitan Government Bureau of Waterworks, Headquarters for Corruption Prevention (2012). *Report on the Results of the Examination of Corruption Prevention Measures in the Bureau of Waterworks* (in Japanese). https://www.waterworks.metro.tokyo.lg.jp/files/items/20407/File/hokokusho.pdf (viewed May 27, 2022).

176 Sustainability Management and Network Management

Tokyo Metropolitan Government Bureau of Waterworks, Headquarters for Corruption Prevention (2014). *Report on the Results of the Examination of Measures to Prevent Corruption, etc. at the Bureau of Waterworks* (in Japanese). https://www.waterworks.metro.tokyo.lg.jp/files/items/26890/File/hokokusho_h26.pdf (viewed May 27, 2022).

Tokyo Waterworks Group Compliance Expert Committee (2020). *Tokyo Waterworks Group Compliance Expert Committee Interim Report* (in Japanese). https://www.waterworks.metro.tokyo.lg.jp/files/items/27731/File/houkokusyo-200122.pdf (viewed May 27, 2022).

Index

A

accidental misconduct, 164, 172
accidental scandals, 163, 172
activity management, 92–93
administrative control, 15
administrative investigation, 169
affiliation tension, 13
agency theory, 41–42, 45, 51–52
annual SDG awards, 111
augmented reality (AR), 144
average salary per working hour
 (ASPH), 75
awareness of compliance, 171

B

backcasting, 9
balanced scorecard (BSC), 13
belief system, 13, 15
benchmark index, 74
blended value, 57, 63
board of directors, 19, 42–45,
 50–51
boundary system, 13, 15
breakeven time, 144
Brundtland Commission Report, 113
business management system, 10
business model, 4, 6, 10, 30

business model construction, 7
business opportunity, 7
business sustainability, 114

C

carbon, 117
Climate Change Act, 117
climate for inclusion, 126–130,
 133–134
collaborative new product
 development, 142
community, 115
community building, 121
Companies Act, 45, 47, 51
compliance, 162, 170, 174
compliance activities, 163, 173
compliance efforts, 161, 173
compliance program, 164, 174
concept of profit, 56
condition of shared value, 7
content of social value, 5
controlled and low-risk actions, 61,
 66
corporate governance, 19, 163,
 173
Corporate Governance Code, 22
corporate philosophy, 9

corporate scandals, 162–163
corporate social responsibility (CSR),
    46–49, 51–52, 114
corporate value, 174
cost management, 84, 89, 92–94
COVID-19, 80–81, 119
creating shared value (CSV)
    management, 5
customer value proposition, 6

D
declining population, 165
diagnostic control system, 13
difficult but attainable level, 58–59
digital twin, 143
disability, 120
distribution pipelines, 166
diversity, 73
DX, 81
dynamic simulations, 145, 155

E
economic, 113
economic value and social values, 5
ecosystem, 122
effectiveness of collaboration, 10
employee engagement, 12
engagement, 128–130, 133–134
enterprise value, 96, 98–99, 101–102,
    107–108
environmental pollution, 117
environmental social and governance
    (ESG), 71, 95–99, 107, 114
equity capital, 114
evaluation methods for social value, 5
evaluation of potential profits and the
    sustainability factors, 8
execution tension, 13
expected level, 59–60, 64, 66

F
facility damage, 165
Fair Trade Commission, 169
financial difficulties, 165
financial figure management, 93
financial resources, 122
four perspectives of BSC, 14

G
gender diversity management
    (GDM), 125–130, 133–134
goal congruence, 153, 156
good management theory,
    47–49
governance, 163
governance control, 20, 28
greenhouse gases, 117

H
healthcare, 111
health management, 121
human capital, 122
humanity of employees, 83–84,
    88–90, 93
human resources portfolio, 12
human resources strategy, 11

I
IIRC–PBR model, 97–98, 101
impact weighted accounts
    (IWA), 5
information leak, 164, 169, 173
information leakage, 172
innovative and risky actions, 61,
    65–66
intentional scandals, 162
interactive control system, 13
International Accounting Standards
    Board (IASB), 5

interorganizational tensions, 13
Ito Review, 21, 23

J
Japan SDG Action Platform,
   111
judgment level, 50, 59, 66

K
key performance indicators (KPIs),
   10
KPIs of the business model, 10
Kyocera, 71, 74

L
labor productivity, 73
leadership, 118
learning tension, 13
legal service life, 165
level evaluation, 58–59
local community, 119
local governments, 163, 168
lower permissible limit, 64, 65
lower permissible profit
   limit, 63

M
major earthquakes, 161, 165
management control
   system, 12
market segment, 8
materiality analysis, 9, 14
maximization behavior, 58
maximizing behavior, 56
medical, 121
multi-objective optimization theories,
   56, 62
multiple objectives, 56, 62, 66

N
narrow down, 64, 66
National Health Service, 112
natural capital, 122
natural resources, 118
non-financial capital, 97–98, 102
nursing care, 120

O
operating profit, 76
operating profit per working hour
   (OPH), 75, 80
organizational culture, 15, 163, 173
organizational management, 163
organizational structures, 173
organizational tension, 13
organization for economic cooperation
   and development (OECD), 74
outside directors, 163

P
paradox, 20, 33
per hour labor productivity, 76
pipelines, 161
planet, 120
position within the value network, 8
price book-value ratio (PBR), 80,
   96–102, 104, 107–108
probability evaluation, 58–60, 65–66
productivity indexes, 72
profit equation, 6

R
renewal of pipelines, 168
required level, judgment level, 57
resilient, 118
resolution of economic and social
   tradeoffs, 6

return on assets (ROA), 75–76, 79
return on equity (ROE), 75–76, 79,
   95–98, 101–102, 108
return on sales (ROS), 75–76, 79
revenue, 119
ROESG, 95–98

S
safety management, 174
satisfaction behavior, satisfying
   action, 57
satisfying behavior, 66
satisfying behavior, satisfying action,
   56
scandals, 161, 168, 170, 172–173
semiconductor production equipment
   companies, 96, 98–99, 107–108
shareholder primacy, 45, 47, 51
slack resources theory, 47–49
stakeholders, 161, 168
standard operating procedures,
   60–61, 65
Stewardship Code, 23
stewardship theory, 41–42, 51
stock indexes, 74
structure of the corporate value chain,
   8
sustainability, 111, 161, 170, 174
sustainability activities, 11
sustainability goals, 9
sustainability manager, 11
sustainability measures, 14
sustainability-oriented activities, 10
sustainability-oriented decisions, 11
sustainability-oriented models, 7
sustainable corporate value
   improvement, 11
sustainable development, 113

sustainable development goals
   (SDGs), 71, 111, 164
sustainable management, 40–41, 43,
   45, 51–52
sustainable supply chain, 141–143
synergistic effects between economic
   value and social value, 5

T
talent management, 12
target level, 58
target pricing, 147
time labor productivity, 71
top management, 39–41, 43, 49, 51
Toyota Production System (TPS), 83
tradeoff curve, 62, 65, 67
turnover intention, 129–131,
   133–134

U
United Nations (UN), 111

V
value-added, 72
value and social value, 4
value balancing alliance (VBA), 5
value-based pricing, 147
value chain, 8
value network, 8
value proposals, 8
value proposition, 8
virtual reality (VR), 144
visual information sharing, 145

W
waste, 118
water leakage, 165
water pipelines, 165

water supply revenues, 161, 167
Waterworks Law, 167
waterworks utilities, 161–162, 165,
    167–168, 170–171, 173–174
welfare, 120

Welfare and Medical Health Agency,
    114
well-being, 73, 118
willingness to pay, 150
work reform system, 72

Printed in the United States
by Baker & Taylor Publisher Services